Test Driv
Development

Gojko Adzic

Test Driven .NET Development with FitNesse
Gojko Adzic
Copy-editor: Marjory Bisset
Cover picture: Brian Samodra

Published 2008
Copyright © 2008 Neuri Limited

Neuri Limited
25 Southampton Buildings
London WC2A 1AL
United Kingdom

You can also contact us by e-mail: contact@neuri.com

Register your book online

Visit http://gojko.net/fitnesse and register your book online to get free PDF updates and notifications about corrections or future editions of this book.

ISBN: 978-0-9556836-0-2 REVISION:2008-02-18

Acknowledgements

This book is a result of a small independent publishing effort, and as such would not be possible without the help of many people.

In first place, I would like to thank my technical reviewers Andy Glover, Chris Roff, Cory Foy, Mike Stockdale, Naresh Jain and Ryan McCullough. Many thanks for many excellent suggestions — your comments really made this book much better. I guess I need to thank Mike Stockdale once more for creating FitNesse.NET and giving me such a wonderful subject for the book.

Marjory Bisset from Pearl Words did a great job as the copy–editor of this book; thank you for the many hours you spent correcting my grammar and making the book easier to read.

I'd also like to thank the people from Mikro Knjiga publishing company in Belgrade. Without all the tricks I learned while working with you, this book would not have been possible as an independent project.

Bob Stayton from SageHill Enterprises, whom I've never met or exchanged a single e-mail with, has helped me immensely with this book. I could never have prepared this book for publishing without Stayton's instructions on DocBook XSL and his numerous problem-solving messages on the DocBook mailing list. Bob, I feel like I owe you a few bears, and if you are ever in London and want to claim that, please contact me.

Brian Samodra kindly allowed me to use his photograph for the cover picture. Thank you, Brian.

Finally, I'd also like to thank Andy Hunt and Robbie Allen from the Pragmatic Bookshelf for their excellent advice during the early stages of this project. Your help is greatly appreciated.

About the author

Gojko Adzic has been developing software professionally for the last eight years. His programming story so far includes equity and energy trading, mobile content delivery, e-commerce, on-line betting and complex configuration management.

He has also been involved in several IT newspapers and magazines, with more than 200 published articles about programming, operating systems, Internet and new technologies, and held the position of Editor-in-Chief of PC World in Serbia for two years.

Gojko is currently based in United Kingdom, where he helps companies build better software.

To get in touch, write to gojko@neuri.com or visit www.gojko.net.

Part I. Getting started

In this part of the book, we prepare for our journey. The first chapter introduces FitNesse and test driven development. In the second chapter, we set up FitNesse and go through a quick test to make sure that everything works OK before moving on to the real thing.

Chapter 1.

Introduction

Test-driven development (TDD) really shook the world of software development from the very foundations, much more than any other extreme programming idea. Ten years ago it may have been some sort of mystical programming skill only known to true kung-fu masters. Today, it is becoming common sense, practised even by teams that do not follow any agile methodology.

Whether test-driven development should or should not be done is no longer an issue, but there is still an issue about how best to do it. This book is about doing test-driven development in a .NET environment better, with the help of two great open source tools: FIT and FitNesse. These tools allow us to apply TDD principles efficiently and improve communication with customers and business analysts. FIT and FitNesse help all team members build a shared understanding and effectively speak the same language.

Who should read this book?

This book is primarily aimed at .NET developers interested in starting with TDD and those who already practise unit testing and want to move beyond that into development driven by acceptance testing. It will also be useful to Java developers who are experienced with FitNesse, but wish to use it in a .NET environment. The .NET and Java implementations differ significantly in some ways, and this book points out all the important .NET-specific features. Java developers can also benefit from the third part of this book, where we discuss best practices for using FitNesse in a team environment and integrating FitNesse into the wider software development ecosystem, including web and database tests.

You will learn how to write and manage tests effectively, how to integrate FitNesse into your development process, and how to extend it to meet particular project needs. You will learn when to use FitNesse, when not to use it, and when to combine it with unit testing tools. You will also discover how to get customers to help out with testing and how to use FitNesse to make project requirements clearer.

Why bother with TDD?

If you bought this book to learn about test-driven development, then you are probably wondering how a single practice can have such a big impact on our work. In defence of my statement that TDD is now common sense, here is a brief overview of what it can do for us.

Before the rise of test-driven development, testing and coding were traditionally two separate activities. Programmers would write code and forget about it. Quality Assurance people tried to flush out as many bugs as they could before the release. From time to time, the software would be so bug-ridden that the QA engineers had to pull the plug. Sometimes things got even worse: a system would be delivered still full of bugs and customers would besiege the support staff with angry calls and e-mails. Problems never started out big, but they were allowed to grow between coding and testing.

TDD was a conceptual shift from this practice, spreading testing over the entire development process. Problems are not allowed to grow. Guided by the "test early, test often" principle, we do a bit more work up front, but that significantly reduces the effort required to support the code.

The following quotation from "Competing on the Basis of Speed",[1] a presentation given by Mary Poppendieck at Google Tech Talks on the 15th of December 2006, summarises the benefits of TDD very effectively:

> When we started up in our plant...
>
> ...we had people in QA who used to try to find defects in our products, and we moved them all out on to the production line to figure out how to make stuff without defects in the first place...You will be amazed at how much faster you go when you make stuff and defects are caught when they occur instead of being found later.
>
> —Mary Poppendieck

TDD allows us to work amazingly fast, because it improves the whole process in several ways.

---

[1] http://video.google.com/videoplay?docid=-5105910452864283694

Quality from the start

TDD keeps problems small. Because tests take place early in the development process, rather than late, problems surface quickly and get solved before they grow. We can build quality into our products right from the start.

Early interface validation

The only way to know if an API makes sense is to use it. TDD makes developers eat their own dog food because tests are effectively the first API client. If the API does not make sense or if it is hard to use, the developers experience this first hand. Tests should be easy to write, and if they are not, then we need to change the code to make testing easier. This makes it easier for other people to use our code.

Divide and conquer

In order to test code modules in isolation, developers have to divide them into small independent chunks. This leads to better interfaces, clear division of responsibility, and easier management of code.

Safety net for the code

At the beginning of development, changes to software are quick and simple. As the code base grows, it becomes harder to modify. A simple change in one area often causes problems in a seemingly unrelated part of the code. Without tests, it soon becomes too hard and expensive to change anything. When we test all parts of the code, problems are quickly identified wherever they are.

Confidence = Productivity

As craftsmen, most developers take pride in their work and want to deliver quality software. Making changes to production code when we are not confident in the quality feels like walking on broken glass. Having tests tell us that we are on the right track, allows us to be more confident in our work and enables us to change the code faster.

Light at the end of the tunnel

Tests can be an effective way to describe specifications and requirements. If used properly, they can guide the development process, showing us what we need to implement. Once all tests pass, the work is done. This light at the end of the tunnel makes it easier to focus on the development effort.

Beyond unit tests

One of the main goals of this book is to help people move beyond unit tests. However, please understand that *this is not a book against unit testing*. Unit testing is an incredibly useful practice and I am not trying to make a case against it. However, it has become a victim of its own success. Because NUnit and similar tools are now so ubiquitous, they get abused by being used for component and integration tests or even for acceptance testing. These tools were never designed for such tasks. The role of tests has evolved from verifying functionality to guiding development, and for this we need a completely different set of tools. Useful as they are, unit tests are often not enough.

Back in 2002 I worked on configuration management software. That beast had more edge cases than anything I had seen before. The whole team wasted enormous effort on manual verification. About the time that we started to rewrite the engine in Java, I read about JUnit, which came like a gift from heaven. We automated most of the dull verification tasks. Problems became smaller and we were no longer wrestling with big issues that required several days to diagnose.

A few months later, I could no longer understand how I ever managed to work without unit testing. Putting requirements into tests turned out to be a great way to make sure we all agreed on the targets, and provided us with guidelines on how to hit them. Tests provided an early sanity check for our APIs. JUnit was magic.

Our software was used by sales teams in several large electrical equipment manufacturers. The software provided the ability to instantly validate any configuration — for example, a particular motor with a particular power supply. It also automatically provided a price quote, a delivery proposal, and a bill-of-materials list. Rules for an average product took about a month to model and probably about two more months to test and clean up. Hierarchical dependencies and connections made the models very error-prone. People from the modelling department were really not at ease with making any changes after the initial version was approved. We solved this issue in our code, so we thought that we could do the same for the models. We developed a glue between JUnit and configuration models, which would theoretically allow someone to write and automate tests for models. This practice never advanced from a proof-of-concept stage. Configuration modellers did not know Java, did not want to know it, and could not be bothered to work in an IDE. They could not read JUnit tests nor understand what went wrong if something failed.

Step by step, I started to see other limitations of unit tests. The target we set with JUnit was our vision of the goals, which was not necessarily the same as the client's vision, and there was absolutely no way we could get clients to read and verify the tests. JUnit was great for small pieces of code, but quite cumbersome when external systems were involved, especially when there was work to be done in the database. Knowing what I know now, I really wish I had had FitNesse in mid-2003.

Getting FIT

Framework for Integrated Testing (FIT) is an acceptance testing framework originally developed for Java by Ward Cunningham. One of the central ideas of FIT was to promote collaboration and allow customers and business analysts to write and verify tests.

FIT makes it easy to run tests, but does not provide a way to create them. The original idea was to write tests in Word, Excel, or any tool that can output HTML. FitNesse is a web wiki front-end to FIT developed by Robert Martin and Micah Martin from ObjectMentor. Today, it is the most popular choice for running FIT tests. It provides an integrated environment in which we can write and execute tests and speeds up the job with quite a few useful shortcuts.

Although FitNesse was also written in Java, it was not heavily integrated with FIT, but executed it as an external program. This turned out to be a very good idea, as it was possible to plug in different test runners. After the FIT/FitNesse combination became popular in the Java world, test runners were written for other environments including C++, Python and .NET. The .NET integration was developed by David Chelimsky and Mike Stockdale; version 1.0 was released in late 2006. Judging from its success in the Java world, FitNesse will soon become one of the most popular tools for .NET test-driven development.

How does FitNesse help?

Writing FIT tests does not require any special programming knowledge or technical proficiency. Modellers who could not use JUnit if their life depended on it can write tests with FitNesse without any problems. A typical FitNesse test is shown in Figure 1.1: test inputs and expected results are specified in a table, with expected outcomes having a question mark in the column. The tables can be written in Excel, Word or any HTML editor. FitNesse even provides a special wiki syntax to build tables more efficiently than in plain HTML. This tabular form makes it very easy to write tests and view results.

Figure 1.1. A typical FIT test table

Forex rates as of 2008-03-10				
Currency	USD rate?	EUR rate?	GBP rate?	JPY rate?
USD	1.00000	0.73188	0.49633	115.721
EUR	1.36635	1.00000	0.67816	158.116
GBP	2.01479	1.47457	1.00000	233.154

FIT tables connect to the domain code using a very thin fixture code layer, which is effectively more an integration API then a testing API. FIT requires very little extra code for testing, but just enough to provide a sanity check for the underlying interfaces. Often, FIT fixtures constitute the first client of our code.

FitNesse is a web-based server, allowing easy collaboration. Business analysts and other non–technical people do not have to set up any software in order to use FitNesse. Any browser will do just fine. Additional documentation, project notes, diagrams and explanations can be easily bundled with tests in FitNesse, providing deeper insight into the problem domain and helping people understand and verify test results. All this helps to evolve tests along with the code.

FIT and FitNesse are much better than unit testing tools for getting non–technical people involved with the testing process, especially in defining and verifying acceptance criteria. They allow developers to turn requirements and email conversations into tests almost instantly. Business analysts and managers can read the tests, verify results and track progress.

Testing rules are decoupled from the code, so tests can easily evolve along with the business rules. This also allows us to write tests before any code, even before the interfaces, without breaking the build. FitNesse tests are also a good way to pass requirements to external developers and teams; they act as a technical specification of what needs to be done.

FitNesse or NUnit?

As a relative newcomer to the arena of .NET test tools, FitNesse inevitably gets compared to NUnit. So let's tackle this issue now.

The primary target of FIT and FitNesse are customer-oriented acceptance tests, and that is where these tools really excel. NUnit and similar tools are aimed at code-oriented tests, verifying the functionality and the design of software from the developer perspective. However, the ease of writing and managing complex tests with FitNesse makes it also attractive as a tool for code-oriented tests.

The most important technical difference between NUnit tests and FitNesse (FIT) tests is that FitNesse tests are, for the most part, not in the code. They are described with HTML tables and run from an external server. This coin has two sides: it is easy to write FitNesse tests even before we start coding (so tests can truly guide the code), and half-done tests will not break the compilation. On the other side, FitNesse tests are somewhat harder to debug, and are not automatically refactored with the code.

Unit tools are excellent for testing code, but they suffer from a domain mismatch when we try to describe something outside of their basic language. Writing database or UI tests in C# can be quite inconvenient. With FIT/FitNesse, database tests can be described in a tabular form and UI tests in a story-like list of instructions.

Instead of splitting tests between NUnit and FitNesse by whether they are code-oriented or customer-oriented, I think that a more useful criterion is the area of coverage.

Quick basic tests: use NUnit

All developers should run basic tests (and make sure that they work) before committing code to the main branch. The basic test suite is normally executed a few times until all the obvious bugs are solved. So these basic tests have to run as fast as lightning, and they have to run on developer machines. Such tests typically do not connect to real services, but use mock objects to simulate the workflow. They should test small parts of the code, focusing on mistake-proofing in the small. In two words: unit tests.

From my experience, any unit test suite that runs longer than a minute is more of an obstacle than an aid. People will start skipping tests, which pretty much defeats the whole point of having them. This does not mean that we should not write tests that run longer, just that people should not be made to run them every time (see section *"Don't mix quick and slow tests"* on page 111). Michael Feathers summarised a discussion on the XP mailing list on a similar subject in this way:[2]

> A test is not a unit test if
>
> - It talks to the database
> - It communicates across the network
> - It touches the file system
> - It can't run at the same time as any of your other unit tests
> - You have to do special things to your environment (such as editing config files) to run it
>
> Tests that do these things aren't bad. Often they are worth writing, and they can be written in a unit test harness. However, it is important to keep them separate from true unit tests so that we can run the unit tests quickly whenever we make changes.
>
> —Michael Feathers

It works well to keep *true* unit tests in a tool like NUnit, so that we can run them from within the IDE. Note the word *true*: component and integration tests in disguise are not welcome here. Using NUnit makes basic tests easier to debug and troubleshoot, giving us a quicker turnaround time between spotting a problem and fixing it.

Manageable larger tests: use FitNesse

FitNesse has quite a few useful features that make tests easier to write and manage than with a unit-test tool. This is why I recommend keeping larger code-oriented tests in FitNesse, in addition to acceptance tests. Categorising tests like this also enables us to execute component and integration tests separately from the basic test suite, and not worry too much about their speed. They can then connect to real services, a proper database, and check larger and longer workflows.

FitNesse is miles better then unit-test tools for regression tests (see Chapter 13, *Testing legacy code*). The tabular language for describing tests in

---

[2] http://www.artima.com/weblogs/viewpost.jsp?thread=126923

FitNesse makes it a good choice for relational data tests and database testing (covered in Chapter 12,*Testing database code*). Also, FitNesse integrates nicely with various libraries, like Selenium for web user interface testing (covered in Chapter 11,*Testing web interfaces*).

Because of its descriptive language, FitNesse can help to turn e-mails about bug reports into automated tests quickly. It is also a good tool for getting non–developers involved in the process of testing; it is much easier to get support people to write a FitNesse test than a NUnit test.

Not a silver bullet

FitNesse is not a general solution to all testing problems. For example, FitNesse does not support record-and-replay operations, which are a very effective way of automating GUI tests. It is also not a good tool for load testing and performance testing.

As explained in the previous section, FitNesse is not a replacement for unit testing tools, but is an addition to them. Think of it as a bigger hammer, which can also work on smaller nails, but is better used when you need more power and best combined with other tools when you need more precision.

Having said all this, FitNesse is an extremely useful utility in its own domain. It is an ideal tool for writing and managing story tests, the testing complement of user stories, which have become the preferred way of collecting requirements in agile teams. FitNesse truly helps in setting the target for development, making sure that everyone involved agrees what the target is, and automating verification to check how the development is going.

The next step

In the next chapter, you will install FitNesse. After that, in the second part of the book, you learn about key features of FitNesse while developing an application guided by TDD principles. In the third part of the book, you investigate how best to use FitNesse in a team environment. You also learn how to expand tests to cover more than just .NET code, crossing the borders into web user interfaces and databases.

Stuff to remember

- FitNesse provides many shortcuts for efficient test writing.
- No programming knowledge is required to write FIT tests.
- The tabular view makes tests easy to write and results easy to read.
- FIT requires very little extra code.
- An online server enables the whole team to contribute to testing.
- Documentation can be bundled easily with tests.
- Customers, business analysts and managers can understand and verify FitNesse tests.
- Tests can be written before any code.

Chapter 2.

Installing FitNesse

FitNesse is a great tool for collaboration and testing, and has many nice features that will help us work more efficiently and produce better software. Unfortunately, an easy installation is not something FitNesse can boast, at least not for a .NET environment.

FitNesse works in combination with several software tools and frameworks, which you'll have to download and install separately. So, in order to set up a working server, you must get your hands a bit dirty, but the effort will be well worth it. Before diving into the world of automated testing, you'll need to set up everything and run a quick sanity check to make sure that your new tool is working correctly.

FitNesse is a web application with its own server written in Java. It uses a .NET version of FIT test runner (a Windows .NET executable) internally to execute .NET tests. The test runner must be downloaded separately. So, to use FitNesse for testing .NET code, you need:

- Java VM 5 or 6 to support FitNesse. Download and install from http://java.sun.com.
- Microsoft .NET 2 (at least) Framework to support FIT.NET. Download and install from http://msdn.microsoft.com/netframework.
- FitNesse server. Download the latest release from http://www.FitNesse.org/FitNesse.DownLoad. The file you should look for has a name similar to `fitnesse20070619.zip`. FitNesse.org occasionally goes down for maintenance. If it is not accessible when you try to download the latest release, go to the alternative download site http://www.fitnesse.info/download.
- FIT.NET binaries for .NET 2. Download the latest release from http://sourceforge.net/projects/fitnessedotnet.

Setting up FitNesse

There is no special installation procedure for FitNesse. Just unpack the zip archive downloaded from FitNesse.org somewhere on your disk. Depending on the release, the archive may contain a `dotnet` folder, but this either contains a .NET 1 test runner (in versions before 20070619) or is just empty (in version 20070619). So you also need to unpack the .NET

2 test runner. I suggest opening a dotnet2 folder in the main FitNesse folder, and putting FIT.NET there. This path is used in the examples in this book. If you put .NET 2 runner somewhere else, remember to change the path in code examples. After you have unpacked and moved items as described, your installation directory should look like the one shown in Figure 2.1.

Figure 2.1. FitNesse files and folders

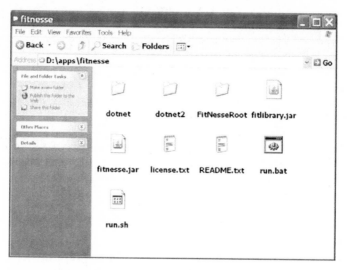

The package you just downloaded contains some very useful examples for Java, but do not rely on them too much, nor on the user guide provided in the package. FitNesse.NET integration has quite a few differences from the Java version and the official user guide is completely Java-oriented.

Start FitNesse by executing **run.bat** from the main FitNesse folder (either via command line or double-click). FitNesse works as a web application with its own web server and tries to open port 80 by default. If this port is already taken on your machine, open **run.bat** in any editor and add **-p 8888** to the end of the command before executing it. You can replace 8888 with some other free port on your system. I use 8888 in the examples, so if you use another one, remember to enter the correct port when you try out the examples. The changed file should look like this:

```
java -cp fitnesse.jar fitnesse.FitNesse -p 8888 %1 %2 %3 %4 %5
pause
```

When FitNesse starts, you should see a command window with this message:

```
FitNesse (20070619) Started...
port:   8888
root page:  FitNesse.wiki.FileSystemPage at ./FitNesseRoot
logger:   none
authenticator: FitNesse.authentication.PromiscuousAuthenticator html page
factory:  FitNesse.html.HtmlPageFactory
page version expiration set to 14 days.
```

Run.bat failed. What's wrong?

Read the exception from the command window. If the error mentions versions, check that you have Java 5 or 6 installed and that the correct version is being executed when you run **java.exe**. Run **java.exe -version** from a command window to see which version of Java is being executed by default. You can run FitNesse with a different Java version either by pointing to the correct JVM in the system executable path (right-click **My computer** , select **Properties**, then go to **Advanced** tab, click **Environment Variables**, and edit the **Path** variable), or by entering the full path to a different **java.exe** in **run.bat**.

If the error report states that there is a security problem or the port is unavailable, enter a different port number in **run.bat** and try again.

If the error report is "Unrecognized option: -p", you must have added **-p 8888** before the java class name, so put it after other options.

Open http://localhost:8888/ and you should see the welcome page (Figure 2.2).

FitNesse is up and running. When you want to shut it down later, just press **Ctrl+C** in the command window (or close the command window).

A quick test

In order to verify that everything works correctly, let's write a quick test. To make the first example as simple as possible, we will not test a business object but the string concatenation operator. To test whether it works, we will join the words "Hello" and "World", put a blank in between, and check that the result is "Hello World". In the process, we write a simple test page in FitNesse, bind that test page to .NET code and make FitNesse run .NET tests. We will first create and run this test example very quickly, but then go back and work through the details.

Figure 2.2. FitNesse welcome page

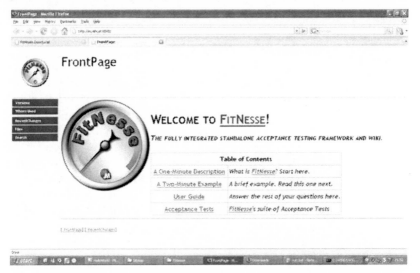

FIT is the engine driving FitNesse, responsible for executing tests. It reads HTML files, looks for tables, and uses data in the tables to execute tests and compare results to expectations. FitNesse is a wiki[1] site with helpful mark-up shortcuts, designed to help with building the test pages.

FIT requires a thin integration layer on top of our code, which provides hooks to the methods and properties of business objects so that they can be mapped to test data and expected results. This integration layer typically consists of a set of classes derived from fit.Fixture, or some of its standard subclasses.

Open a new .NET project, and copy this class into it (without the line numbers):

---

[1] A web-based content management system, typically intended for collaborative use, allowing people to create and edit pages easily using a simple mark-up syntax. Wikipedia is a popular example, which you have almost certainly seen by now, so working with FitNesse should not feel strange.

For full code, see HelloWorld/HelloWorld.cs on page 175

```
1   namespace HelloWorld
2   {
3     public class OurFirstTest : fit.ColumnFixture
4     {
5       public string string1;
6       public string string2;
7       public string Concatenate()
8       {
9         return string1 + " " + string2;
10      }
11    }
12  }
```

Add a reference to fit.dll (in the dotnet2 FitNesse folder) to your project and compile it.

Now open http://localhost:8888/HelloWorld in your browser. You should see a screen telling you that there is no *HelloWorld* page and offering a link to create a new page. Click on the link and FitNesse opens the page editor: a big text box with several buttons. Now type the following code into the text box (without the line numbers) and click **Save**. Make sure to replace the DLL path with the full path to your project's DLL.

For full code, see HelloWorld on page 202

```
1   !define COMMAND_PATTERN {%m %p}
2   !define TEST_RUNNER {dotnet2\FitServer.exe}
3   !path D:\work\fitnesse\HelloWorld\bin\Release\HelloWorld.dll
4
5   !|HelloWorld.OurFirstTest|
6   |string1|string2|Concatenate?|
7   |Hello|World|Hello World|
```

FitNesse now creates a new page and displays it (Figure 2.3). Next, you have to tell FitNesse that this is a test page — click **Properties** on the left, check the **Test** check box (Figure 2.4), and click **Save Properties**. Page properties define what the user can do with the page — more precisely, which buttons will be offered in the left-hand menu.

Figure 2.3. FitNesse creates a new page for the Hello World test

Figure 2.4. Remember to mark the page as a test

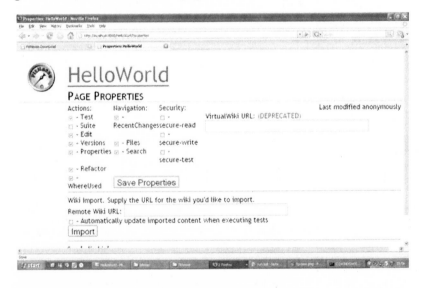

When the page reloads, you will notice a new button on the left: **Test**. Click it to make FitNesse run the test. You should see a page similar to Figure 2.5, telling you that the test passed.

Figure 2.5. Our first test passed!

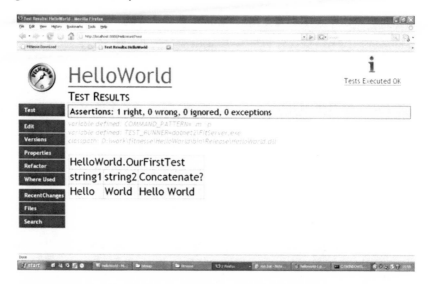

OK, that was our first FitNesse test in .NET, and it passed. Hurrah! Now let's go a few steps back and see what really happened.

My test was all yellow – what have I done wrong?

- Double-check the path to your DLL. Due to some strange Java-Windows issue, the DLL name is case-sensitive.

- Check that the test class and its methods and fields are public.

- Check that the method and field names match the table header.

- Check that there is an exclamation mark before the first row.

- Check that there is a question mark after Concatenate in the second row of the table.

- Check that you put FitServer.exe into the dotnet2 folder under the main FitNesse directory (the one where you started run.bat from).

How FitNesse connects to .NET classes

By default, FitNesse executes Java tests, so the first thing we have to do is make it run .NET tests. The first two lines in our test page tell FitNesse to use the test runner from the dotnet2 folder:

```
!define COMMAND_PATTERN {%m %p}
!define TEST_RUNNER {dotnet2\FitServer.exe}
```

The third line specifies the location of test classes:

```
!path D:\work\fitnesse\HelloWorld\bin\Release\HelloWorld.dll
```

Then comes the test table. FIT uses tables to describe both the tests and expected results, and binds these tables to our code. Tables may seem like a strange choice at first, but this turned out to be a very good idea. Rick Mugridge explains[2] that tables provide just enough structure to organise information properly, without getting in the way. The tabular form also allows test report and feedback to be given in the same form as the tests, which makes FIT and FitNesse easy to use. You have probably already worked out that in FitNesse you create a table by entering rows (lines) in which you separate cells with the pipe symbol (|). The first line of the table tells FitNesse which class to load (and how to execute the test):

```
!|HelloWorld.OurFirstTest|
```

FitNesse automatically converts *CamelCase*[3] names into page links, but in this line HelloWorld.OurFirstTest is a test class name, not a page link. The exclamation mark before the first cell in the table header tells FitNesse not to convert it to a page link. It is good practice to put an exclamation mark in front of the table even if the class name is not in CamelCase form.

The test class extends ColumnFixture, which maps public fields, properties and methods to columns. When you use ColumnFixture, the second row of the table should contain field, property or method names:

```
|string1|string2|Concatenate?|
```

---

[2] see page 28 of Fit for Developing Software[2]
[3] Two capitalised words joined together. See section *"FitNesse is very strict about the page names"* on page 22.

All subsequent rows are data rows: they contain parameter values and expected results:

```
|Hello|World|Hello World|
```

Each data row in a `ColumnFixture` table defines one test execution. Notice that both parameter values and expected results appear in the same row. Columns that define an expected outcome have a question mark after the method name. Fields and properties can also be used to check expected outcomes in the same way. If a column header does not end with a question mark, FitNesse uses the corresponding data in the next row as test input, setting the parameter or field value. If the column header does have a question mark, the method is executed or the current field or property value is read, and the result is compared to cell contents. So, the first data row in our table would be equivalent to the following NUnit test code:

```
HelloWorld h=new HelloWorld();
h.string1="Hello";
h.string2="World";
AssertEqual("Hello World",h.Concatenate());
```

Here's an interesting experiment. Edit the test page (click **Edit** on the left), add a new data row with a wrong value in the expected results column, then run the test again. This time, the test fails (Figure 2.6), clearly marking a problem both in the page header and in the table. Test results show both the expected and actual value for the failed test, so you can quickly see what went wrong.

Don't forget the test

The new test is now available on http://localhost:8888/HelloWorld and you can browse to this URL at any time to repeat the test. However, URLs like this are easy to forget, especially when you start writing more tests. Luckily, FitNesse has a feature that makes it easier for you to find tests later. Go to the home page of the test site, click **Edit**, and add **HelloWorld** anywhere in the page. Save the page and when it reloads, you will see a link to the "Hello World" test.

FitNesse automatically converts CamelCase names into links, and all test pages in FitNesse should have CamelCase names (which is why we called the test *HelloWorld*). You can even add a link before you create the page: FitNesse displays a question mark next to the link and allows you to build the new page. When the page is finally created, the question mark disappears.

Figure 2.6. Failed tests are clearly marked – and both actual and expected values are displayed

FitNesse is very strict about the page names

If you created a page (or tried to create one) and got a NullPointerException error, or the page is just not appearing, you chose a wrong name. FitNesse considers only CamelCase words as valid page names and is strict about this. The page name must start with a capital letter and contain at least one more capital letter. There is one more issue to watch out for: consecutive capital letters. FitNesse does not like them. So the capital letters in a page name must be separated by at least one lower-case letter. This convention causes a lot of headaches to FitNesse newbies, but after a while you'll get used to it. Here are some good page names:

- HelloWorld
- TestFluxCapacitor
- IsPaymentWorkingCorrectly

Here are some page names that will get you in trouble:

- helloworld (no capital letters)

- Testfluxcapacitor (just one capital letter)
- isPaymentWorkingCorrectly (starts with a lower-case letter)
- TestFCapacitor (two consecutive capital letters)

Playtime

Here's some stuff to try on your own:

- Fix the test in Figure 2.6.
- Create a class that counts words and characters in a string, then write a ColumnFixture wrapper and a test page to verify that it works correctly.

Stuff to remember

- In order to connect to .NET projects, you have to tell FitNesse to use a .NET test runner (FitServer.exe) and specify the path of your project DLLs.
- We describe tests in tables containing both test parameters and expected results.
- The table header specifies the test class name.
- Put an exclamation mark at the beginning of every table to protect table data from wiki formatting.
- If a test fails, FitNesse shows both expected and actual outcome.

Part II. FitNesse and TDD in practice

In this part we find out how FitNesse can make our work easier by developing an application. In doing so, we explore key features of FitNesse and apply TDD practices and principles to produce better software.

The task ahead of us is a (very) simplified version of a real application I worked on while I was learning how to use FitNesse in a .NET environment. (As they say in the movies, names and places have been changed to protect the innocent.) Although we go through just one iteration of the application, we will stumble upon all the obstacles my team experienced with FitNesse and find out how to overcome them.

Chapter 3.

Our Project

Let's build an online lottery system. Imagine that our client is a lottery operator from Tristan da Cunha, and they want to open their lottery to the world.[1]

Lottery rules

The lottery operator organises weekly draws, in which punters pick six out of forty possible balls. All the money from lottery tickets goes into the *draw pool* before the draw. The lottery operator takes a large part of the money for operational costs and the rest is divided amongst the winners. (Money available for prizes is called the *payout pool*). Several prizes are allocated from this pool, typically grouped by the winning combination. So, for example, 68% of the payout pool is reserved for people who guess correctly all six numbers — they all get a share of the 6-out-of-6 prize. All the winners in the 5-out-of-6 category share 10% of the payout pool, and so on.

Our task is to develop a system that will enable players to purchase tickets and participate in lottery draws. Players will have an online account where they will be able to deposit money with their credit card or by wire transfer. All winnings will be paid into this account automatically when the operator enters draw results into the system , and the players will be able to spend money from the account to buy new tickets or withdraw the money by wire transfer. The operators will typically offer draws for the next two months online.

Selected user stories

After a short discussion with the customers, we agree that our first iteration should include the following stories:

Calculate expected winnings

As an operator, I want the system to display expected winnings, so that players will be enticed to buy tickets.

---

[1] Tristan de Cunha is the most remote inhabited archipelago in the world. They probably don't have Internet access or a local lottery on the island, but with a bit of imagination, this application will serve well as an example. See http://en.wikipedia.org/wiki/Tristan_da_Cunha.

Register player

As an operator, I want players to register and open accounts before purchasing tickets, so that I have their details for marketing purposes and to prevent fraud.

Buy tickets

As a player, I want to buy tickets so that I can participate in lottery draws and win prizes.

Pay out winnings

As an operator, I want the system to locate the winning tickets, calculate winnings and pay money into ticket holders' accounts when I enter draw results.

View tickets

As a player, I want to view my tickets, so that I can find out if I have won and how much.

We implement these stories in the following chapters, writing functional and acceptance tests as we go along.

Applying TDD to our project

Test-driven development is just a set of simple practices supported by a few lightweight tools, most of which are free. On the surface, these practices and tools aim to improve the quality of software with more rigorous and more efficient code checking. However, that is just the tip of the iceberg. There is much more to TDD then verifying code. As the name suggests, in test-driven development, tests play a proactive, leading role in the development process, rather than the reactive role of checking software after it is written.

Guiding the development

A strict implementation of a feature with TDD consists of three stages:

1. Write a test for the feature and write just enough code to make the test compile and run, expecting it to fail the first time.
2. Change the underlying code until the test passes.

3. Clean up the code, integrate it better with the rest of the system and repeat the tests to check that we have not have broken anything in the process.

This sequence is often called *"red-green-refactor"* or *"red bar-green bar-refactor"*. The name comes from the status icon or status bar in most GUI test runners, which is red when tests fail and green when they pass.

User stories

In the last few years, user stories have emerged as the best way to collect requirements and guide deliveries for agile projects. Stories are different from use cases in their focus on customer benefit: each story should ideally describe a system behaviour that brings value to the users. A typical story template is "as a *role*, I want *behaviour*", ideally with an additional "so that *benefit*". This is not a book on writing user stories, so I'll keep this block short. If you are interested in learning more about the subject, I suggest you read *User Stories Applied* by Mike Cohn [7].

Stories are important for this book because they are a natural starting point for defining acceptance tests. Acceptance tests based on user stories are called *story tests*. Because each story describes a system behaviour with direct impact on the customer, not one wrapped in layers of technical abstractions, business analysts and customers should easily be able to define how to check whether the system behaves as they expect. A good starting point is the question "how do we verify that this story has been implemented correctly and completely?"

Even if you are not using an agile methodology, identifying such key system behaviours and talking to the customer about how to verify that they are correctly implemented is good practice. You can then use these validations as a target for development and a signal to tell you when the job is done.

Requirements change as the project moves on, as concepts and ideas mature. As a general rule of thumb, it is best to discuss how to verify a story in detail just before it is scheduled to be developed.

Once the first test passes, we write another test, write more code, make the new test run, clean up again and retest. After we have repeated this cycle for all the tests for a specific feature, our work on the feature is done and we can move on to the next feature. Robert C. Martin summarised this connection between tests and production code in his *Three Rules of TDD:*[2]

The Three Rules of TDD

Over the years I have come to describe test driven development in terms of three simple rules. They are:

1. You are not allowed to write any production code unless it is to make a failing unit test pass.
2. You are not allowed to write any more of a unit test than is sufficient to fail; and compilation failures are failures.
3. You are not allowed to write any more production code than is sufficient to pass the one failing unit test.

—Robert C. Martin

This approach may seem too strict or radical at first. Additional tests are often written after the first version of the code has been developed. Some people write the code first, then do the tests and modify the code until all the tests pass. This technique also works, as long as the tests are written in the same development cycle as the code, and extra care is taken to focus on the user stories, not the code.

Think about the intention, not the implementation

A test is pointless as a quality check for the code if it just replicates what the code does. Any bugs that found their way into the code will just be replicated in the test. Tests that just replicate code are very dangerous because they will give you a feeling of comfort, thinking that the code is tested properly, while bugs are waiting round the corner. Do not write the test by looking at the code, as you may get blinded by the implementation details. This is one of the reasons why it is better to write tests before the code, not after.

Tests that guide the development should always reflect the intention, not the implementation.

If you are just getting to know TDD, I strongly recommend doing it first by the book, as described above. Once you get accustomed to practices

---

[2] http://butunclebob.com/ArticleS.UncleBob.TheThreeRulesOfTdd

and underlying principles and see how they fit into your particular way of working, you can optimise and adjust the process.

Automated acceptance testing

Although the three rules of TDD deal with unit tests, they apply equally to tests that operate on a much larger scale. Iteration goals and business rules can also be translated into automated tests and used to help programmers focus their development effort. Tests that describe these goals are known as *acceptance tests* or *customer-oriented tests*. They do not focus on the code, but on the customer's expectations. Unit tests check whether the code does what programmers wanted it to do. Acceptance tests check whether the product satisfies the customer's requirements. In the same way that unit tests act as a target for code functionality, acceptance tests act as a target for the whole project. So, the first step of development is to ask business analysts or customers how we can verify that the code we are about to write works correctly. Having the acceptance criteria written down helps to flush out any inconsistencies and unclear requirements. Having the criteria in the form of an automated test makes it easy to check that we are on the right track.

The name "acceptance test" is a bit misleading. When used properly, an acceptance test is more a specification for development than a test. Naresh Jain suggested that I should use *"executable specification"* instead of "acceptance test" in this book. I like that name much more because it truly reflects the role of acceptance tests in modern programming, and clears up a lot of questions that I often get. In spite of being misleading, "acceptance test" is an established name for this concept, and I decided to stay with it in this book. However, keep in mind that we are actually talking more about specifications than tests.

Who should write acceptance tests?

Acceptance tests should reflect the customers' perception of when the system meets requirements, so they must be defined by a customer or a business analyst. This still leaves us with the question of who should translate this definition into FitNesse tables. There was an interesting discussion on this topic at the XPDay 2007 conference in London, during a workshop called "Working With Customers towards Shared Understanding". Several participants noted that if developers are left to write acceptance tests on their own, the tests turn out too technical and task-oriented. Acceptance tests are more effective if they are focused on larger activities and expressed in the language of the business domain. Although FitNesse allows customers and business analysts to write tests directly without involving developers, that may be a step too far. Customers often forget about edge cases and focus only on general rules. Antony Marcano, one of the maintainers of TestingReflections.com, pointed out that discussions between developers and customers during test writing help a lot to clarify the domain and enable developers to understand the problem better. If tests are written by customers on their own, then the value of these discussions is lost. So, ideally, a developer and a customer representative, or a business analyst, should write the tests together.

Is it better to use acceptance or unit tests?

When acceptance tests drive the development, large parts of the production code are covered by these tests. Some people tend to write fewer unit tests because acceptance tests already check the functionality. Although this practice does save some time, it may make it harder to pinpoint problems later. Failed acceptance tests signal that there is a problem, but do not locate the source as clearly as unit tests do. Acceptance tests also rarely check edge cases so unit tests have to be written at least to cover those issues. Infrastructural parts of the code, not especially related to any user story, will also not be properly covered with acceptance tests.

In my experience, it's best to use both unit and acceptance tests. One group does not exclude the other. If this question bothers you, ask it again but use executable specification instead of acceptance test. You need both the specification and tests for your code, and should not choose between one of them.

Looking at the bigger picture, James Shore offers his *"Describe-Demonstrate-Develop"* best practice for using FitNesse:[3]

Describe-Demonstrate-Develop

Now I draw a very sharp distinction between FIT and TDD. I use FIT at a higher level than TDD. If TDD is "red-green-refactor", then my use of FIT ("Example-Driven Requirements")

---

[3] http://www.jamesshore.com/Blog/How-I-Use-Fit.html

is *"describe-demonstrate-develop"*. The "develop" step includes all of TDD.

1. *Describe.* In the FIT document, use a short paragraph to describe part of the functionality that the software supports. (This should be done by business experts.)
2. *Demonstrate.* Provide some examples of the functionality, preferably examples that show the differences in possibilities. Sometimes only one or two examples is enough. (This should be done by business experts, too, possibly with help from testers and programmers.)
3. *Develop.* Develop the functionality using TDD. Use the structure and terms of the examples to provide direction for the domain model, per Eric Evans' Ubiquitous Language. Turn each kind of concept in the examples (such as "Currency") to drive the creation of new types, per Ward Cunningham's Whole Value. (This should be done by programmers.) Don't run FIT during this stage until the small increment of functionality is done. When it is, create the FIT fixture and hook it up. Use your Whole Value classes rather than primitive types. When you run FIT, the examples should pass.
4. *Repeat.* Continue with the next section of the document. Often, the business experts can go faster than the developers and finish several more Describe/Demonstrate sections before the programmers finish Developing the first section. That's okay and I encourage that they do so. There's no need for the business experts to wait for the programmers to finish Developing a section before the business experts Describe and Demonstrate the next one.

As you expand the FIT document, you should see opportunities to reorganize, change, and improve sections. Please do. You'll end up with a much better result.

—James Shore

Testing to prevent defects, not to find them

TDD brings into the software world a lot of ideas from *zero quality control* (ZQC), Toyota's approach to achieving product quality. Understanding the principles of ZQC and applying them while writing tests can significantly improve the effectiveness of TDD.

The basic idea of zero quality control is that quality has to be built into the product, and does not come from controlling and sorting out defects at the end. Toyota's solution consists of a design approach that aims to create mistake-proof products and uses successive inexpensive tests to detect problems at the source.

Poka-Yoke, or mistake-proofing, is one of the most important principles of zero quality control.[4] It is an approach to manufacturing that aims to prevent problems by either making products error-proof by design or by providing early warning signals for problems. Although Toyota made these practices famous, other designers have been applying them for quite a while. For example, any average elevator checks the load before departing and stops working if it is overcrowded. Some also give a clear warning using a flashing light or sound. This is how an elevator stops a potential problem by design.

Poka-Yoke design

The Poka-Yoke design approach seeks to prevent problems by making products less prone to misuse. *"A Brief Tutorial on Mistake-proofing, Poka-Yoke, and ZQC"* by John R. Grout and Brian T. Downs[5] is a good introduction to ZQC, and contains some very interesting examples from everyday life.

Monitor cables are a common example of Poka-Yoke design. The connectors are asymmetric, so that it's obvious how to plug them in. Of course, with the right application of brute force, cables can be plugged in wrongly, but it is much easier to use them correctly. Grout and Downs also mention the interesting example of fire alarms that cannot be fitted on to the ceiling if a battery is not installed. Another very interesting example given by Grout and Downs is the Bathyscaphe Trieste,[6] a deep-sea submersible used to explore the ocean bed. Normally, if there was an electrical failure, anyone inside such a vehicle would be doomed. However, when Poka-Yoke desgn methods are applied, the submersible's ballast silos are held by electromagnets, so that an electric failure causes the craft to start rising to the surface immediately.

---

[4] see http://gojko.net/2007/05/09/the-poka-yoke-principle-and-how-to-write-better-software/ for a more detailed discussion of how Poka-Yoke applies to programming.

[5] http://csob.berry.edu/faculty/jgrout/tutorial.html

[6] http://en.wikipedia.org/wiki/Bathyscaphe_Trieste

Checking at the source, rather than at the end, was one of the most important ideas described by Shigeo Shingo (1909-1990) in his book on zero quality control [8]. Mary Poppendieck often comments on the idea that "inspection to find defects is waste, inspection to prevent defects is essential".

On production lines, the mistake-proofing principles are applied using Poka-Yoke devices: test tools used to check, inexpensively, whether a produced item is defective. Poka-Yoke devices enable the workers to identify problems straightaway on the manufacturing line. They allow quick and cheap checking, so that they can be used often to verify the quality at different stages.

Software tests and testing tools are our Poka-Yoke devices, allowing us to check quickly whether procedures and classes are defective, straight after we write them. Tests are automated so that they can be quickly and effectively executed later to confirm that the code is still working.

Exterminating bugs

Nothing makes a developer look more incompetent than bugs that reappear. We can use TDD tools to make sure that dead bugs stay dead.

Ideally, every time someone finds a bug, a developer or support engineer should write a test to confirm it. This will help us aim at the right target while solving the problem and make sure that the bug is fixed. It will also help us to check whether the bug has resurfaced in the future.

This also holds for suspected bugs. If you have any doubts about the functionality in an edge case, you can remove it by writing a quick test. Tests to check for bugs are different from red-green-refactor tests because they are written after the code, based on expected problems arising from a particular implementation. Such tests should be written to break the code intentionally.

The next step

In the next chapter, we will take a detailed look at a basic FitNesse test. Then in Chapters 5 to 9 we'll focus more on practical features and problems than on technical details — you'll find out how best to write test scripts, how to organise and manage groups of related tests, how to save time and effort by using specialised test types and how to combine various test classes to get the best effect.

Since this book is about test-driven development and not about how to build .NET applications in general, we focus mostly on the test classes, not on the classes being tested. The primary aim with the application we develop is to demonstrate and try out features of FitNesse, not to build a production-quality system, so we will sacrifice some best practices in the code for the sake of clarity and simplicity. We will also skip over less important parts of the code. However, should you want to dive deeper into the rest of the code, download it from the book's website http://gojko.net/fitnesse or see the full listings in Appendix D, *Source code*.

Stuff to remember

- First write a test that fails, then write code to make it pass, then clean up and retest.
- The first step in development is to describe acceptance tests that define when the work is done.
- Test to prevent defects, not to find them.
- Guidance tests should always reflect the intention, not the implementation.
- Unit tests focus on the code, acceptance tests focus on customer benefits.
- When you hear "acceptance test", think about "executable specification".

Chapter 4.

Writing basic tests

In Chapter 2,*Installing FitNesse*, you had a brief introduction to FitNesse tests. Now is the time to take a deeper look at the bridge between test and domain code. In this chapter you also learn why FitNesse tests are more understandable than unit tests. Our task for this chapter is to implement the first user story:

> Calculate expected winnings
>
> As an operator, I want the system to display expected winnings, so that players will be enticed to buy tickets.

To implement the story, we will write a WinningsCalculator class, which will be responsible for calculating expected winnings for a given draw pool value.

Instead of writing the WinningsCalculator immediately, we take a step back. Remember section *"Guiding the development"* on page 28? The first step of implementation is to decide how we are going to verify that the result behaves correctly. Just to make sure you did not jump over this idea, repeat out loud: *The first step of implementation is to decide how we are going to test the result!* And we need to agree on that with someone from the business side, to be sure that the result is really what they want. So, after a short discussion with our business analysts, we decide that the best way to test the winnings calculator is to take the results from the last month's draw (Figure 4.1), put the pool size into the calculator and check whether the numbers match.

Figure 4.1. Last month's results

Winning combination	Pool allocation	Value
Total pool	100%	$4,000,000
Payout pool (PDP)	50%	$2,000,000
6 out of 6	68% of the PDP	$1,360,000
5 out of 6	10% of the PDP	$200,000
4 out of 6	10% of the PDP	$200,000
3 out of 6	12% of the PDP	$240,000

Write the FitNesse page before you write code

In order to explain the syntax of various FitNesse tables in this book, we typically write the fixture code first and then look at how that code maps to FitNesse tables. But once you learn what those fixtures can do for you, it is actually much better to create the FitNesse page first and let that lead you while writing the fixture class and changing the underlying business interfaces.

Writing the FitNesse test page first will allow you to make sure that programmers and customers have the same understanding of the problem. Keep working on the FitNesse pages until both you and the customer think that you have sufficient examples to start programming.

Test-driven development by the book advocates writing the test before we actually write the production code whenever possible. The test then serves as a target for development. So, let's write just enough of the WinningsCalculator class to be able to compile the test. We need to test two things: calculating the pool percentage, and calculating the prize pool.

For full code, see Tristan/src/InitialWinningsCalculator.cs on page 179

```
1   namespace Tristan
2   {
3     public class WinningsCalculator
4     {
5       public int GetPoolPercentage(int combination)
6       {
7         throw new Exception("Not implemented");
8       }
9       public decimal GetPrizePool(int combination, decimal payoutPool)
10      {
11        throw new Exception("Not implemented");
12      }
13    }
14  }
```

ColumnFixture – the Swiss Army knife of FitNesse

The section *"A quick test"* on page 15 touched upon the subject of the thin integration layer built on top of business code that FIT requires. This is the integration class fit.Fixture, which provides hooks to relevant properties and methods of business objects and tells FIT how to run the test. Although fit.Fixture is always the base class for all integration classes, it does not specify how to run the test. Instead, we typically extend a subclass of Fixture for our tests. In the rest of the book, we'll call such subclasses *fixtures*. There are many ready-made fixtures in the basic FIT package (fit.dll) and the popular extension FitLibrary[1] (fitlibrary.dll). Also, you can develop your own fixtures to extend the functionality of FitNesse (see section *"Implement domain-specific tests using custom fixtures"* on page 160) so there are quite a few candidates to choose from. Which fixture class should we use in this case?

To test the WinningsCalculator class, we need to check that the allocated percentage of the payout pool and prize value are correct for all winning combinations (and a given value of the payout pool). If the test is a calculation, described in the form of "check that results are correct for given inputs" and there are a few known inputs to try out, we should use ColumnFixture as the base for the integration class.

What else can I use ColumnFixture for?

The ColumnFixture class can be used to perform almost any test. It can also be used to set up data for other tests and execute methods to clean up after the tests. In fact, ColumnFixture is so easy to understand and use and can be used in so many situations, that it is like a Swiss Army knife for FitNesse tests.

ColumnFixture is a good choice if the same tests should be repeated for a specified number of different combinations of input parameter values. When you don't know the number of tests in advance, or there is only one check to perform, there are better solutions that can save you a lot of time and effort. These solutions are described in later chapters.

The fixture class should allow us to define the total value of the payout pool and the winning combinations, and check allocated percentages and prize pool values. So let's create two properties for the inputs and two methods to calculate results:

---

[1]FitLibrary is a set of extensions developed by Rick Mugridge, now considered part of the standard set of fixtures, although it is technically a separate library. The FIT.NET package already contains the FitLibrary, so you do not have to download it separately. We use FitLibrary fixtures in Chapter 6, *Writing efficient test scripts* and Chapter 8, *Coordinating fixtures*.

For full code, see Tristan/test/PayoutTable.cs on page 188

```
1    namespace Tristan.Test
2    {
3      public class PayoutTable:fit.ColumnFixture
4      {
5        private WinningsCalculator wc=new WinningsCalculator();
6        public int winningCombination;
7        public decimal payoutPool;
8        public int PoolPercentage()
9        {
10         return wc.GetPoolPercentage(winningCombination);
11       }
12       public decimal PrizePool()
13       {
14         return wc.GetPrizePool(winningCombination, payoutPool);
15       }
16     }
17   }
```

Wait a moment... are those public fields?

Yes! It is bad practice to expose public fields in API classes, but PayoutTable class is not a part of the API; it will be used just for testing.

Using public fields in test classes makes them easier to write and read. We often use public properties in test classes in this book, to keep them short. Anyway, if you are picky about this issue, go ahead and implement them as properties or setter methods, FitNesse will not care.

Now we write the test page. Add a link to *PrizeCalculation* from the home page (as explained in section *"Don't forget the test"* on page 21), then click this link and create a new page. Add the three setup lines, described in section *"How FitNesse connects to .NET classes"* on page 20, defining the test runner and location of the project DLL. Make sure to enter the correct path to DLLs on your system; it may differ from the one in this book.

The table for ColumnFixture tests has at least three rows: the first row specifies the fixture class name, the second names input and output methods and properties, and the following rows specify test data and expected results. In this case, payoutPool and winningCombination are inputs, and methods PoolPercentage and PrizePool calculate output values. (Fields and properties with a getter can also be used for test outputs.) To differentiate between inputs and outputs, `PoolPercentage` and `PrizePool` end with a question mark in the second row. Parentheses () can also be used to specify outputs, but to keep things consistent when properties are used for outputs, and to make tables easier to read, I recommend that you just use the question mark. Rows after the second row just contain last month's draw results. Here is the table that you should copy into the page:

For full code, see PrizeCalculationFirstTry on page 205

```
4   !|Tristan.Test.PayoutTable|
5   |payoutPool|winningCombination|PoolPercentage?|PrizePool?|
6   |2000000|6|68|1360000|
7   |2000000|5|10|200000|
8   |2000000|4|10|200000|
9   |2000000|3|12|240000|
```

Save the page, then tell FitNesse that this is a test page (using page properties). You can run the test by clicking **Test**. Because we have not yet written the whole `WinningsCalculator` class, the test fails. Now that we have a clear understanding of what the class should do, let's write it to satisfy the test.

For full code, see Tristan/src/WinningsCalculator.cs on page 179

```
1   namespace Tristan
2   {
3     public class WinningsCalculator
4     {
5       public int GetPoolPercentage(int combination)
6       {
7         switch(combination) {
8           case 6: return 68;
9           case 5: return 10;
10          case 4: return 10;
11          case 3: return 12;
12          default: return 0;
13        }
14      }
15      public decimal GetPrizePool(int combination, decimal payoutPool)
16      {
17        return payoutPool * GetPoolPercentage(combination) / 100;
18      }
19    }
20  }
```

Recompile the project, run the test again, and it passes (Figure 4.2).

Figure 4.2. Winnings Calculator works!

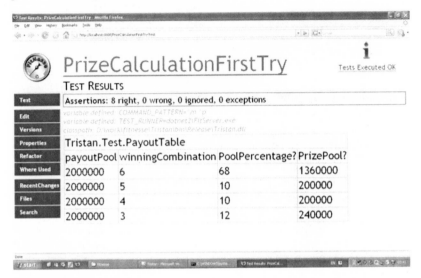

Testing in plain English

Having written this test, you might wonder why this is any better than using NUnit. We have written almost as much code as we would have to write for NUnit, and it is not any more readable to non-programmers than the NUnit test would be.

FitNesse is not just for unit testing. In fact, it is not intended for unit testing at all, although it can be quite good for describing functional tests. The primary target of FIT and FitNesse are acceptance tests — turning what the customer actually wants into tests and automating them. And yes, the table does not look any better than a NUnit test right now, but this is just the beginning.

One of the original goals of FIT was to enable non-technical users to collaborate on writing tests. Several syntax tricks and a bit of smart formatting can make test pages much more readable and closer to the English language than to C#. Here are a few tricks to start with.

Use names that are easy to read − FitNesse will find the correct .NET equivalent

When mapping tables to classes, properties, variables and methods, FitNesse does a case-insensitive search and ignores blanks. So, instead of:

```
|payoutPool|winningCombination|PoolPercentage?|PrizePool?|
```

we can write:

```
|Payout Pool|Winning Combination|Pool Percentage?|Prize Pool?|
```

The test looks much better on the screen, is easier to read, and splitting names into several words solves the problem of automatic CamelCase conversion into links.

Import namespaces and clean up table headers

To make the test class header simpler, remove the namespace, and import it using the `Import` table. Start the table with a single word: `import`. Then specify namespaces in the following rows.

```
!|import|
|Tristan.Test|
```

We need to import the namespace only once for the entire page (actually, once for the entire test suite, which I'll explain later). We can even divide the class name into several words.

Replace repetitive values with arguments

The payout pool in your test is always the same, and repeating it in every table row just clutters up the screen. You can initialise it once for the entire table by using *fixture arguments*. Rather like the `Main` method of a console application, a fixture can have a number of optional string arguments, which are stored in a protected array `Args`. So we can change the class to read the payout pool from a fixture argument:

For full code, see Tristan/test/TotalPoolValue.cs on page 198

```
12    public decimal? payoutPool;
13    public decimal PrizePool()
14    {
15       if (payoutPool == null) payoutPool = Decimal.Parse(Args[0]);
16       return wc.GetPrizePool(winningCombination, payoutPool.Value);
17    }
```

Specify arguments in the first row of the test table, after the class name.

FitNesse cannot find the Import table – why?

The `import` command is, in fact, a special test table defined in `fit.dll`. Although the online documentation does not mention any specific preconditions for the import command, some versions of the .NET runner do not automatically include standard test classes. If FitNesse cannot find the `import` table, add a line containing

```
!path dotnet2/fit.dll
```

to the start of the page. This will make sure that the basic FIT library is included in the search for fixtures.

Talk to the customer

Generally, we can call our test classes and variables anything we like, so let's use this flexibility to make sure the customer also understands what is going on. Let's rename the test class to make it more understandable to the customers, for example, "Prize Distribution for Payout Pool".

Use comments to describe tables

Any text outside of tables is just ignored. You can write explanations, include images, provide links to more information, or modify the test pages in any way you feel would improve understanding. This is one of the best features of FitNesse. Most testing frameworks do not allow for the provision of varied contextual information easily. So, let's add a short description of what this test does, to make it even clearer.

What if I want to provide a table with additional details?

FitNesse executes all tables as tests, but there is a simple solution for providing non-test tables. Just put Comment as the table header and the table will be ignored. Comment is actually a test class that does nothing.

Use .NET formatting to make values easier to read

Counting those zeroes on the screen is really not fun. Big numbers are pretty ugly, but FitNesse uses .NET number formatting internally, which enables us to use separators for digit groups. For example, we can specify the pool size as 2,000,000 instead of 2000000.

Customer-friendly table

The end result in Figure 4.3 looks much like the original winnings table in Figure 4.1. If we could only insert the dollar sign, it would look exactly like the table. This can also be done easily, but let's leave the gold-plating for later (see section *"Simplify verifications with a custom cell handler"* on page 158).

Figure 4.3. This table looks much more customer-friendly

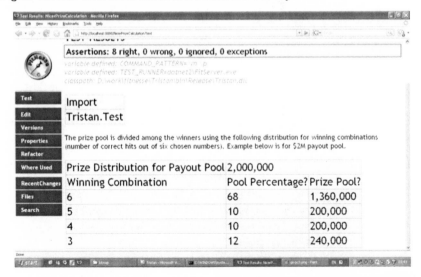

The clients and business analysts should have no problem understanding the results and verifying that the system actually does what they want. The business analysts can now use the page to discuss and review the requirements if and when the clients change their minds, and we can run automated tests and easily check what works and what is broken.

Playtime

Here's some stuff to try on your own:

- Use properties with a getter instead of methods for test outputs.
- Use properties with a setter instead of fields for test inputs.
- Modify the tests to use the total pool value (before operators take their cut) for input instead of the payout pool value.

Stuff to remember

- Write FitNesse pages first, and use them as a target for the production code.
- Use `ColumnFixture` when you want to repeat the same check for several different combinations of input values.
- The `ColumnFixture` class maps properties, methods and fields to table columns.
- You specify that a column contains expected results by ending the column name (in the second row) with a question mark.
- A table can have more than one column for expected results, enabling us to perform several verifications for the same combination of input values in a single table row.
- FitNesse allows you to use names that are easy to read. It finds the correct .NET equivalent by joining words and ignoring character case.
- Any text outside of tables is just ignored, so you can provide explanations and comments along with your tests and make them easier to verify and understand.
- If you want non-technical people to understand and verify tests, then you should make sure the test tables are as close as possible to their natural language.

Chapter 5.

Writing simple test scripts

Tests are rarely as simple as the one described in Chapter 4, *Writing basic tests*. Generally, they involve several steps and verifications. FitNesse allows us to write multi-step test scripts as easily as simple verifications. In this chapter we develop the next story, and learn how to write test scripts and pass values between tables. Our task for this chapter is to implement the second user story:

Register player

As an operator, I want players to register and open accounts before purchasing tickets, so that I have their details for marketing purposes and to prevent fraud.

Again, we speak to our business analysts about what to test and how to verify that the story has been implemented correctly. The first thing they say is that, upon successful registration, personal details should be stored correctly in the system and the player should be able to log in with their registered username and password. Also, the balance for new accounts in the system should always be zero.

Focus on fixture code

To keep things simple, we will focus on test fixtures and test-specific code in this and the following chapters. Business classes will be discussed just enough to support the story. You can see the implementations of these classes in Appendix D, *Source code*. You can also download them from http://gojko.net/fitnesse.

To implement the story, we need to allow players to register and log in. Each player will have a unique numeric ID, which should be returned from the registration method (let's call it RegisterPlayer) if the operation is successful. Let's create a data-transfer interface where we will store all the personal details of the player required for the registration — we will call it IPlayerRegistrationInfo. The LogIn method should return the corresponding player ID, if the username and password are correct. If not, an exception is thrown. We also need a way to retrieve player details to verify that they are stored correctly.

So, let's create a `PlayerManager` class, responsible for managing players in our system. To begin with, we give it this API:

For full code, see Tristan/src/IPlayerManager.cs on page 177

```
30        int RegisterPlayer(IPlayerRegistrationInfo p);
31        IPlayerInfo GetPlayer(int id);
32        IPlayerInfo GetPlayer(String username);
33        int LogIn(String username, String password);
```

Passing values between tables

The test that we need to write for this chapter actually involves a few stages:

1. Register a new player.

2. Check that user details were stored correctly and that the balance on the new account is 0.

3. Try to log in with the username and password provided during registration.

Although everything could be described by one (huge) table, the resulting test page would be completely unreadable, which defeats the whole point of using FitNesse. We can put more than one table on a single page and they will be executed in sequence. This allows us to create a test script that describes the steps with small and focused tables.

Use setup fixtures to store static context

Once we divide the test into several tables, we have to handle issues associated with their interdependence. The first one is that the tables must work with the same `PlayerManager` instance. A typical solution for sharing this kind of information between tables is to use a separate fixture to set up the test environment.

This setup fixture stores the contextual information into static properties. (There is also a standard fixture class called `SetUpFixture`, which will be explained in section *"Use SetUpFixture to prepare the stage for tests"* on page 83 . In this case, we are talking about generic setup fixtures that prepare the stage for other fixtures, not necessarily of any particular class). Let's call this class `SetUpTestEnvironment`.

For full code, see Tristan/test/PlayerRegistration.cs on page 189

```
6     public class SetUpTestEnvironment : Fixture
7     {
8       internal static IPlayerManager playerManager;
9       public SetUpTestEnvironment()
10      {
11        playerManager = new PlayerManager();
12      }
13    }
```

This class would typically be responsible for initialising service objects, connecting to the database, and anything else our test environment requires to run correctly. In the example we extend fit.Fixture directly, because no parameters are being passed to the class. When you need to pass connection strings or other setup information, you can use any other fixture class. ColumnFixture is a good candidate.

Use symbols to pass dynamic information

Static values and singletons[1] are fine for storing resources that we can anticipate while writing the FIT integration class, like database connections and service objects. However, tables in the same script often have to share dynamic information. By dynamic, I mean values created on the fly in the tests. For example, we might write a table that registers a new player, and another one that verifies that the player data was stored correctly. The second table needs to know the ID of the player created by the first table. If we were to use a static variable for this, the two test tables would be coupled quite strongly. As soon as we need to perform checks on two players, we would have to modify the registration test class code and add another static variable, making the verification class even more complex, as it would need a switch to indicate which variable to use as the ID.

A better solution for passing dynamic information between tables is to use FitNesse *symbols*. Symbols are global variables that can be accessed using a simple syntax. To store a value of an output column into a symbol named player, write >>player into the cell. To read a symbol value, and store it into an input column, use <<player. Think of << and >> as arrows pointing the way.

---

[1] A design pattern that restricts classes to only one instance, see http://en.wikipedia.org/wiki/Singleton_pattern

What is the scope of a symbol?

Symbols are stored in a static collection inside the Fixture class, so their scope is global from the point where they are defined until the test runner stops. So far, we have only executed a single page at a time, so the scope of a symbol is from its first use until the end of the current page. You will learn how to run multiple pages within a single test runner in section *"Group related tests into test suites"* on page 71

A symbol scope will effectively extend to all pages executed after the page where it is defined. However, do not count on sharing symbols between pages because the order of page execution is not guaranteed — it is best to define and use the symbol on the same page.

Writing a simple test script

Let's first check the registration. We start with the bare minimum, user-name and password, and add other personal details later. Building on the skills gained with the previous story test, we write two ColumnFixture classes: one to register a player and one to verify the stored username and new account balance.

For full code, see Tristan/test/PlayerRegistration.cs on page 189

```
17    public class PlayerRegisters : ColumnFixture
18    {
19      public string Username;
20      public string Password;
21      public int NewPlayerId()
22      {
23        PlayerRegistrationInfo reg = new PlayerRegistrationInfo();
24        reg.Username = Username;
25        reg.Password = Password;
26        return SetUpTestEnvironment.playerManager.RegisterPlayer(reg);
27      }
28    }
29    public class CheckStoredDetails : ColumnFixture
30    {
31      public int PlayerId;
32      public string Username
33      {
34        get
35        {
36          return SetUpTestEnvironment.playerManager.
```

```
37                    GetPlayer(PlayerId).Username;
38            }
39      }
40      public decimal Balance
41      {
42         get
43         {
44           return SetUpTestEnvironment.playerManager.
45             GetPlayer(PlayerId).Balance;
46         }
47      }
48    }
```

To check whether a player can log in, we can wrap the `PlayerManager.LogIn` method into a `bool` function.

For full code, see Tristan/test/PlayerRegistration.cs on page 189

```
49      public class CheckLogIn:ColumnFixture{
50         public string Username;
51         public string Password;
52         public bool CanLogIn()
53         {
54           try
55           {
56             SetUpTestEnvironment.playerManager.LogIn(Username, Password);
57             return true;
58           }
59           catch (ApplicationException)
60           {
61             return false;
62           }
63         }
64      }
```

Now we can write the test tables, simply connecting them with symbols. In order to make the test more customer friendly, use keywords *yes* and *no* instead of true and false in test tables. Remember to add the setup for .NET test runner and your DLL path.

For full code, see PlayerRegistrationFirstTry on page 203

```
9    !|Set Up Test Environment|
10
11   !|Player Registers|
12   |username|password|new player id?|
13   |johnsmith|test123|>>player|
```

```
14
15  !|Check Stored Details|
16  |player id|username?|balance?|
17  |<<player|johnsmith|0|
18
19  !|Check Log In|
20  |username|password|can log in?|
21  |johnsmith|test123|yes|
```

Notice that FitNesse shows actual values next to symbol names when the test is executed (Figure 5.1), enabling us to review what really went on during the test run.

Use ready-made classes to set symbol values

Symbols can also be used to parameterise tests. For example, when you know that a certain value might change in the future, store it into a symbol and use the symbol in tests. When the value changes, you need to update it just in one place.

You can use a set of very useful classes from an internal FitNesse test suite to manipulate symbols directly. They are: StringFixture, IntFixture, DoubleFixture, LongFixture, BoolFixture, FloatFixture and DecimalFixture. All these classes manage symbols of the corresponding type, and have a field called Field that you can use to set and test symbol values. Here is an example that puts "Vogon Constructor Fleet" into a symbol named what:

```
!|StringFixture|
|field|field?|
|Vogon Constructor Fleet|>>what|
```

The first column sets the value of the internal Field inside String-Fixture. The second column puts the current Field value into the symbol.

Use data-transfer objects directly

Mapping columns to properties becomes quite cumbersome with more complex objects. In real-life projects, domain packages probably already have a good *data-transfer object* (DTO), so this direct mapping just complicates test classes unnecessarily. FitNesse allows us to use a data-transfer object directly without declaring all its properties in a fixture class. In order to do that, we override the GetTargetObject method of the Fixture class to specify our DTO. In this case, we use the PlayerRegistrationInfo class,[2] which implements the IPlayerRegistration data-transfer interface.

Figure 5.1. Registration tests - first attempt

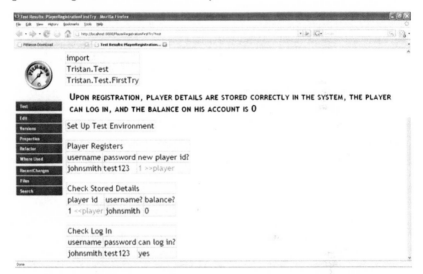

When GetTargetObject is overriden, the fixture class tells FitNesse how to execute tests, but does not directly provide the test implementation. For example, our fixture can just tell FitNesse to execute a ColumnFixture test, but the target object has to implement properties and methods for table columns. When a target object is provided, all table columns must be bound to this object. You cannot mix and match — the whole table is mapped either to the fixture or to the target object. This includes test methods and additional setup columns, which do not exist in the DTO object. I typically solve this by creating an inner class in the fixture that extends the DTO class with test methods.

For full code, see Tristan/test/PlayerRegistration.cs on page 189

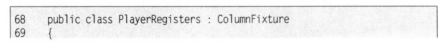

```
68    public class PlayerRegisters : ColumnFixture
69    {
```

---

[2] see section *"Tristan/src/inproc/PlayerRegistrationInfo.cs"* on page 186

```
70    public class ExtendedPlayerRegistrationInfo: PlayerRegistrationInfo
71    {
72      public int NewPlayerId()
73      {
74        return SetUpTestEnvironment.playerManager.RegisterPlayer(this);
75      }
76    }
77    private ExtendedPlayerRegistrationInfo to =
78      new ExtendedPlayerRegistrationInfo();
79    public override object  GetTargetObject()
80    {
81        return to;
82    }
83  }
```

We can use this technique to fill in all the PlayerRegistrationInfo properties without redeclaring them in fixture code, and then use a ready-made DTO as an input for test methods. We can use a similar approach for binding DTO properties to columns that contain expected test results. Theoretically, we could use the same table row to store the player ID and read other properties into the DTO, but this would require copying values from one DTO object to another. The target object can be switched at run time, which is a good way to solve this problem in Java, but because C# inner classes do not have access to outer class instances, this would not be a clean solution. It is much better to use a fixture argument (see section *"Replace repetitive values with arguments"* on page 43) to load the DTO. Sometimes it is quite convenient to use a FitNesse symbol value as the argument, as in this case, because the new player ID is already in a symbol. However, symbols cannot be directly used as arguments.[3] We can pass the symbol name as an argument and read it in the test class, using Fixture.Recall(symbolName). Note that you should not use >> or << in this case, just the plain symbol name.

For full code, see Tristan/test/PlayerRegistration.cs on page 189

```
84    public class CheckStoredDetailsFor : ColumnFixture
85    {
86      public override object GetTargetObject()
87      {
88        int newid=(int)Fixture.Recall(Args[0]);
89        return SetUpTestEnvironment.playerManager.GetPlayer(newid);
90      }
91    }
```

---

[3] There is a patch that provides this functionality, see http://gojko.net/fitnesse.

54

Using symbols to check dynamic values

We can reduce the test code even further. Instead of just checking whether a player can log in, we can use the fact that the login procedure returns a player ID and compare this ID with the stored value. If the cell containing <<symbol is in an input column, as in the first test, the current symbol value is written into the text fixture property. If the cell is in an output column, actual test results are compared to the current symbol value. We can use this to trim part of the code in the CheckLogIn class. Let's change that method to return the actual result of LogIn directly, and then compare it with the player symbol in the table:

For full code, see Tristan/test/PlayerRegistration.cs on page 189

```
92    public class CheckLogIn : ColumnFixture
93    {
94      public string Username;
95      public string Password;
96      public int LoggedInAsPlayerId()
97      {
98        return SetUpTestEnvironment.playerManager.
99          LogIn(Username, Password);
100     }
101   }
```

The new test page can now check for all player properties more easily (see Figure 5.2). The technique of using symbols for comparison can make test results harder to read for customers, so use it cautiously.

Checking for errors

A business analyst comes in with two new requests:

- Can we verify that a player cannot log in with a wrong password?
- Can we verify that a player will not be able to register if the username is already taken?

The .NET FIT runner has a non-standard extension that allows us to check exceptions and errors. Just write error in the cell to signal that an exception should be thrown during the test.

We can even check for a particular exception message or code. In order to do that, we use a different keyword, exception. The syntax is exception[ExceptionType], exception["Exception Message"] (note the quotes) or exception[ExceptionType:"Exception Message"].

Figure 5.2. Registration tests - second attempt

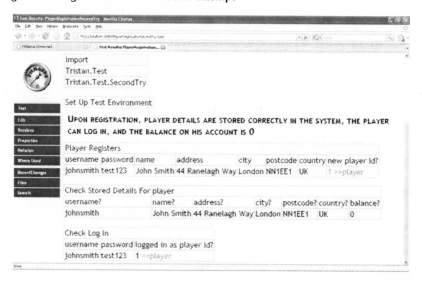

Fixture keywords

In addition to exception, there are a few other fixture keywords you should know:

fail[]   Expects that a comparison will fail - put the expected value in the square brackets. For example, fail[3] will pass if the actual result is not 3.

null   Equal to .NET null. Can be used both as input and for a value check.

blank   Equal to a .NET empty string. Can be used both as input and for a value check.

Note that leaving the cell empty does not automatically check that the result is either null or an empty string. An empty cell makes FitNesse print out the actual result without comparing it to anything, and is a useful trick when you just want to see the result of a method (see section *"Use blank cells to print out results"* on page 143).

Programmers would typically like to check for an exact exception type or message, but this makes tables less readable for business analysts and customers. My advice is to use the level of detail appropriate for the type of test. In customer-oriented tests, error keyword might be quite sufficient. In internal functional tests, full type and message checks provide the greatest level of regression-test safety. A compromise is to use just the exception keyword and a human-understandable[4] message.

Figure 5.3. Registration tests - checking for errors

Note that in Figure 5.3 we have just joined the data rows for two registrations and two login checks. There is no need to repeat the table header each time.

Playtime

Here's some stuff to try on your own:

- Implement a check to verify that username has to consist of at least six and no more than ten letters and digits. No other characters are allowed.
- Register three players and write a test class to verify that their IDs are different (hint: store their IDs into different symbols).

---

[4] Yes, programmers are humans too, but I mean understandable by an average English-speaking human, not someone who has nightmares in C#.

Stuff to remember

- If a page contains several tables, FitNesse executes them in a sequence.
- Symbols are global variables in FitNesse. You can use them to pass dynamic values between tables and connect interdependent tests.
- The current symbol value is shown next to the symbols in test results.
- Use `GetTargetObject` to bind test tables directly to your business class.
- Use `Fixture.Recall` to read a symbol value from your code.
- Use the `error` keyword to verify that an exception is thrown. Use the `exception` keyword to check for a particular exception code or message.

Chapter 6.

Writing efficient test scripts

In Chapter 5, *Writing simple test scripts* we wrote a simple test script, creating a table for each step. When the number of test steps grows, especially if each step is executed only once, the ColumnFixture class no longer seems like a good solution. There is simply too much unnecessary work, both in the class code and in test tables. Now is the time to learn how to write test scripts more efficiently.

Our task for this chapter is to implement the following user story:

> Buy tickets
>
> As a player, I want to buy tickets so that I can participate in lottery draws and win prizes.

Again, the first question to ask is "How do we test that this is done?" Talking to our business analysts, we agree that the story is implemented correctly when the following tests pass:

- A player registers, transfers money into the account and buys a ticket. We need to verify that the ticket is now registered for the correct draw in the system, that the player's account balance has been reduced by 10 dollars, the cost of one ticket, and that the lottery prize fund has increased by the same amount, 10 dollars.
- If the player does not have enough money in the account, the ticket purchase should be refused. The ticket should not be registered, and the player's account balance and the lottery's prize fund should remain unchanged.

This discussion sheds new light on the problem domain. First, we need a way to track active lottery draws and their prize funds and tickets. We create an IDraw interface to represent lottery draws:

For full code, see Tristan/src/IDraw.cs on page 176

```
7    public interface IDraw
8    {
9      DateTime DrawDate { get; }
10     bool IsOpen { get; }
```

```
11      decimal TotalPoolSize { get;}
12
13      ITicket[] Tickets { get;}
14      void AddTicket(ITicket ticket);
15    }
```

Also, we create an ITicket interface to represent lottery tickets:

For full code, see Tristan/src/ITicket.cs on page 178

```
7     public interface ITicket
8     {
9         int[] Numbers { get;}
10        IPlayerInfo Holder { get;}
11        decimal Value {get;}
15    }
```

In order to test ticket purchase, we create a lottery draw and open it. For this, we need a class responsible for keeping track of lottery draws in the system, which also serves as a factory for creating new draws. Call the interface IDrawManager:

For full code, see Tristan/src/IDrawManager.cs on page 176

```
14    interface IDrawManager
15    {
16       IDraw GetDraw(DateTime date);
17       IDraw CreateDraw(DateTime drawDate);
18       void PurchaseTicket(DateTime drawDate, int playerId,
19          int[] numbers, decimal value);
24    }
```

Next, we need to provide a way for players to transfer money into their accounts. Add two methods for this to IPlayerManager:

For full code, see Tristan/src/IPlayerManager.cs on page 177

```
34    void AdjustBalance(int playerId, decimal amount);
35    void DepositWithCard(int playerId, String cardNumber,
36       String expiryDate, decimal amount);
```

DepositWithCard is responsible for general card payment workflow. AdjustBalance is responsible for modifying the actual player balance in the system.

Better test scripts with DoFixture

We discuss the test with our business analysts in a bit more detail, and agree on the following script:

1. Open a lottery draw for 01/01/2008.
2. Player John registers.
3. Player John deposits 100 dollars with card 4111 1111 1111 1111 and expiry date 01/12.
4. Player John buys a ticket with numbers 1,3,4,5,8,10 for the draw on 01/01/2008.
5. Check that the pool value for the draw on 01/01/2008 is now 10 dollars.
6. Check that John's account balance is now 90 dollars
7. Check that a 10-dollar ticket with numbers 1,3,4,5,8,10 is registered for John for the draw on 01/01/2008.

As this test involves depositing money with a credit card, we need to connect our classes to an external payment system. We decide to implement our own test payment system that just allows all transactions. This is an example of a *mock object*, a simple implementation of a component or an external system that allows us to test code more easily.

Column fixtures are great when tests have a repetitive structure, as we can easily add tests by appending data rows to an existing table. However, they are a bit clumsy when dealing with a large data set. Too many columns make a test table unreadable and a column fixture test cannot be split into several rows. Column fixtures are also not ideal when each step of the test is essentially a separate operation. If the script does not have a repetitive structure, we would end up with a separate three-row table for each test step. The solution for all these problems is DoFixture, part of the FitLibrary extension developed by Rick Mugridge.

DoFixture uses a less strict table format and allows test steps to look much like English sentences. Apart from the first row, which specifies the class name, each row executes a single fixture method. Odd cells are joined together to create the method name, and even cells are passed as method parameters. So, for example:

```
| Player | john | buys a ticket with numbers | 1,3,4,5,8,10 |
```

would call method `PlayerBuysATicketWithNumbers`, passing `John` and `1,3,4,5,8,10` as arguments

If the method returns a boolean value, it is considered a test: returning `true` makes the test pass, and returning `false` makes it fail. All other methods are just executed and, unless they throw an exception, they do not influence whether the test passes or fails.

Mock objects can blind you

I'm not a big fan of mock objects. Although they are undoubtedly useful, they can also blind you. A mock object is never implemented to replicate completely and correctly all the constraints of an external system, so it may hide important constraints until very late in the project. In the credit card example, a mock card-service object might hide the fact that expiry date and CVV2 code need to be provided for the real system.

My advice is to use this technique cautiously, and decide whether a mock object is a good solution on a case-by-case basis. When dealing with functional unit tests, mock services are OK because they allow you to focus on a business rule or an important part of the workflow covered by the code unit. With acceptance tests, as a general rule of thumb, try to use an environment as close to production as you can. So if a real payment provider can be used in test mode, I suggest using this instead of a mock payment service. Of course, there are exceptions. Communication with external systems can slow down tests significantly, so it may not always be the best choice.

Catching problems early and continuous integration (see sidebar *"Continuous integration"* on page 116) have proven themselves as two best practices for software development. Don't let mock objects hide problems and cause a big bang integration at the end.

Writing the story in a test table

We can easily rewrite the script as a test table. Let's re-use the test class from Chapter 5, *Writing simple test scripts* to register a player. The rest of the script looks like this:

For full code, see PurchaseTicketFirstTry on page 205

```
18   |Purchase Ticket|
19   |Player|john|Deposits|100|dollars with card|4111111111111111|and expiry
date|01/12|
20   |Player|john|has|100|dollars|
21   |Player|john|buys a ticket with numbers|1,3,4,5,8,10| for draw on |
01/01/2008|
22   |Pool value for draw on |01/01/2008|is|10|dollars|
23   |Player|john|has|90|dollars|
24   |Ticket with numbers|1,3,4,5,8,10| for |10| dollars is registered for
player|john| for draw on |01/01/2008|
```

Now let's write the fixture code. First, we need to change the setup class and add a static IDrawManager resource, so that other test classes can share it. As we need to open a lottery draw, change the setup class to a Column-Fixture class and add a property for opening new draws. Also implement a setter for this property.

For full code, see Tristan/test/PurchaseTicket.cs on page 191

```
8     public class SetUpTestEnvironment : ColumnFixture
9     {
10      internal static IPlayerManager playerManager;
11      internal static IDrawManager drawManager;
12      public SetUpTestEnvironment()
13      {
14        playerManager = new PlayerManager();
15        drawManager = new DrawManager(playerManager);
16      }
17      public DateTime CreateDraw {
18        set
19        {
20          drawManager.CreateDraw(value);
21        }
22      }
23    }
```

Now we'll write the new test class. It has some important differences from the previous test classes, so look at the code closely. First, it extends DoFixture from the fitlibrary package, not from fit like all previous classes. So you might need to add a new reference to your .NET project (use fitlibrary.dll). Second, notice how the array arguments are used: FitNesse automatically converts comma-separated lists of values into an array.

Don't type method names, copy them

DoFixture method names, especially with a large number of arguments, can be a bit hard to type in correctly when you are coding. So don't do it at all: just create a test table and run the test to make it fail. FitNesse then displays an error message to the effect that it could not find appropriate methods and shows you the names it looked for. Just copy and paste them into the class code.

For full code, see Tristan/test/PurchaseTicket.cs on page 191

```
42    public class PurchaseTicket : fitlibrary.DoFixture
43    {
44      public void PlayerDepositsDollarsWithCardAndExpiryDate(
45        string username, decimal amount, string card, string expiry)
46      {
47        int pid = SetUpTestEnvironment.playerManager.
48                      GetPlayer(username).PlayerId;
49        SetUpTestEnvironment.playerManager.DepositWithCard(
50          pid, card, expiry, amount);
51      }
52      public bool PlayerHasDollars(String username, decimal amount)
53      {
54        return (SetUpTestEnvironment.playerManager.
55          GetPlayer(username).Balance == amount);
56      }
57      public void PlayerBuysATicketWithNumbersForDrawOn(
58        string username, int[] numbers, DateTime date)
59      {
60        PlayerBuysTicketsWithNumbersForDrawOn(
61          username, 1, numbers, date);
62      }
63      public void PlayerBuysTicketsWithNumbersForDrawOn(
64        string username, int tickets, int[] numbers, DateTime date)
65      {
66        int pid = SetUpTestEnvironment.playerManager.
67                      GetPlayer(username).PlayerId;
68        SetUpTestEnvironment.drawManager.PurchaseTicket(
69          date, pid, numbers, 10*tickets);
70      }
71      public bool PoolValueForDrawOnIsDollars(DateTime date,
72                      decimal amount)
73      {
74        return SetUpTestEnvironment.drawManager.GetDraw(date).
75                      TotalPoolSize == amount;
76      }
```

```
77      private static bool CompareArrays(int[] sorted1, int[] unsorted2)
78      {
79        if (sorted1.Length != unsorted2.Length) return false;
80        Array.Sort(unsorted2);
81        for (int i = 0; i < sorted1.Length; i++)
82        {
83          if (sorted1[i] != unsorted2[i]) return false;
84        }
85        return true;
86      }
87      public bool
88          TicketWithNumbersForDollarsIsRegisteredForPlayerForDrawOn(
89          int[] numbers, decimal amount, string username, DateTime draw)
90      {
91        ITicket[] tck = SetUpTestEnvironment.
92          drawManager.GetDraw(draw).Tickets;
93        Array.Sort(numbers);
94        foreach (ITicket ticket in tck)
95        {
96          if (CompareArrays(numbers, ticket.Numbers) &&
97              amount == ticket.Value &&
98              username.Equals(ticket.Holder.Username))
99            return true;
100       }
101       return false;
102     }
113   }
```

Figure 6.1. DoFixture script looks like a story

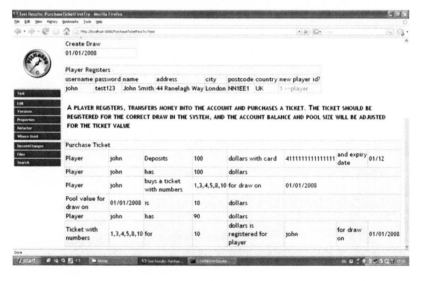

Use DoFixture keywords for better control

Although the test table in Figure 6.1 looks nice, it has one serious flaw. Change the test to check that John has 50 dollars at the end and run it again. You see that the test failed, but not how much money John actually had. If you used ColumnFixture for this, it would print both the expected and actual values. Having this extra bit of information is very helpful for troubleshooting.

DoFixture can do something similar: prefix the row content with check and put the expected value in the last cell. Then change the comparison method to return the actual value, instead of just true/false:

For full code, see Tristan/test/PurchaseTicket.cs on page 191

```
103    public decimal PoolValueForDrawOnIs(DateTime date)
104    {
105        return SetUpTestEnvironment.drawManager.
106          GetDraw(date).TotalPoolSize;
107    }
108    public decimal AccountBalanceFor(String username)
109    {
110      return SetUpTestEnvironment.playerManager.
111        GetPlayer(username).Balance;
112    }
```

Run the test again, and FitNesse displays both expected and actual results (see Figure 6.2). The new comparison method even has a bit less code than the old one.

If you just want to see the result of a method or property value without actually testing anything (equivalent of an empty cell in ColumnFixture), prefix the row with show without appending anything to the end. FitNesse adds a cell to the test results showing the current value.

We can use keywords not and reject to check for errors or failed tests. We can now complete our tasks for this chapter by checking what happens when the player does not have enough money.

For full code, see PurchaseTicketNotEnoughMoney on page 206

```
16   |Purchase Ticket|
17   |Player|john|Deposits|50|dollars with card|4111111111111111|and expiry
     date|01/12|
```

```
18  |reject|Player|john|buys|10| tickets with numbers|1.3.4.5.8.10| for draw
on |01/01/2008|
19  |Check|Pool value for draw on |01/01/2008|is|0|
20  |Check|Account balance for |john|50|
21  |Check|Tickets in draw on |01/01/2008|0|
22  |not|Ticket with numbers|1.3.4.5.8.10| for |100| dollars is registered
for player|john| for draw on |01/01/2008|
```

There is one more interesting DoFixture keyword: note. Prefix a row with
note to turn it into a comment.

Figure 6.2. Use the check keyword to see both expected and actual results in case
of problems

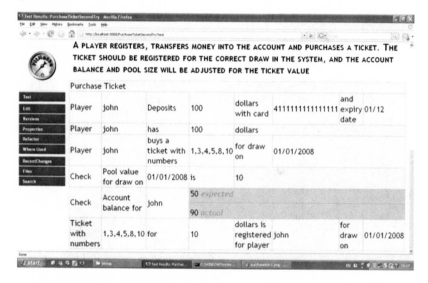

Keep ActionFixture in mind

DoFixture does not currently support checking for a detailed exception
type or error message. If you want this, use ActionFixture instead. Action-
Fixture was originally intended for tests that do not have a repetitive
structure, and it is a part of the basic FIT library. It uses a GUI metaphor
with actions to Enter (set value), Press (call method) and Check (read
value). Some developers like it because it is straightforward and does
not require writing cumbersome method names like PlayerEntersAndIn-
toAndToRegister. DoFixture makes tests much more readable and compact
than ActionFixture, and also has some nice test flow-control features
(discussed in Chapter 8, *Coordinating fixtures*), so generally you should

use DoFixture instead of ActionFixture if you can. However, there are a few cases where you might want to use ActionFixture instead:

- DoFixture does not use FitNesse symbols automatically, and if your tests depend on them, ActionFixture is a much better solution.
- ActionFixture uses the same cell handlers as ColumnFixture, so you can use keywords like fail[], error, or custom comparison expressions like >0, which you cannot do easily with DoFixture. Since release 1.3, you can enable specific cell handlers for DoFixture as well — see tip *"How can I use cell handlers with DoFixture?"* on page 155.
- With ActionFixture, you can check for detailed exception types and error messages (see section *"Checking for errors"* on page 55). DoFixture does not support this yet.

To use ActionFixture, you should not inherit this class directly, but extend fit.Fixture. Put your class name after the keyword start, and then use enter, press and check to define the test. Here is a simple example of a class automated using ActionFixture:

```
class TestConcatenation:fit.Fixture{
  public string FirstString;
  public string SecondString;
  public string Concatenate(){
    return FirstString+SecondString;
  }
  public void Clear(){
    FirstString="";
  }
}
```

Here is the test code:

```
!|ActionFixture|
|start|TestConcatenation|
|enter|first string|Hel|
|enter|second string|lo|
|check|concatenate|Hello|
|press|clear|
|check|first string|blank|
```

Playtime

Here's some stuff to try on your own:

- Add tests to check that a purchase fails if the player selects more or less than six numbers.
- Add tests to check that the purchase fails if the player tries to buy a ticket for a negative amount.
- Write a utility fixture that creates a new player and pays some initial sum of money into the account. Use this in test pages for this chapter instead of the deposit and player registration. Here is a hint:

```
|New Player|john|50|
```

Stuff to remember

- If each step is executed only once, ColumnFixture is not a good solution
- DoFixture is a good choice for test scripts when the steps do not repeat or do not follow the same structure.
- DoFixture rows (if there are no keywords on start) are mapped to methods by joining the content of odd cells, and arguments are defined in even cells.
- DoFixture keywords like check, show and reject change the behaviour of a row if they appear in the first cell.
- Arrays can be passed to fixtures simply by listing members separated by commas.

Chapter 7.

Removing duplication

So far, we have built five or six test pages with quite a few things in common. All the test pages start with the same three lines that define the .NET2 runner and the project DLLs. The test pages in the two previous chapters all include a "Set Up Test Environment" table and some of them also have a common player registration. Repeating the same content in several places is one of the first test smells[1] you should watch out for. We need to remove this duplication and make test pages simpler. This enables us to work faster in several ways:

- If we can avoid repeating boilerplate code, we do not have to worry about getting it right every time.
- Duplicated content may slow us down when we need to change code or adjust tests.
- If the common content is in one place then we can easily change it.

In this chapter, we do not implement a new user story, but take a step back and find out how to organise our tests better.

Group related tests into test suites

So, let's remove the unnecessary duplication. In FitNesse, *subwikis* are the equivalent of web folders or C# namespaces. They can be used to manage related pages more easily as a group. Instead of a slash (/), which is the separator in a web folder name, the dot symbol (.) is used to separate levels of hierarchy in FitNesse.

For example, URL *PurchaseTicketSuite.NotEnoughFunds* leads to the *NotEnoughFunds* page in the *PurchaseTicketSuite* subwiki. Just as a page can be turned into a test with page properties, a subwiki can be turned into a *test suite*. A test suite is a group of related tests that allows us to control their common properties from one place. So, let's create a new test suite with the pages in this chapter.

---

[1] Code smells are symptoms of problems rotting in code, which should be tended to and refactored (See http://c2.com/xp/CodeSmell.html). Martin Fowler attributes the idea of Code Smells to Kent Beck in Refactoring[6]. I use the term "test smells" for similar problems in test pages. See Appendix B, *Test smells* for a list of all test smells mentioned in this book.

First, create the *PurchaseTicketSuite* page, just as you would create any other normal page. You can put the definition of the .NET test runner and your project DLL path there. Instead of defining any test tables, just enter !contents -R as the page content. This automatically builds and shows a table of contents for the subwiki.

For full code, see PurchaseTicketSuite on page 208

```
1   !define COMMAND_PATTERN {%m %p}
2   !define TEST_RUNNER {dotnet2\FitServer.exe}
3   !path D:\work\fitnesse\Tristan\bin\Release\Tristan.dll
4
5   !contents -R
```

There are no subpages yet so the table of contents is blank, but not for long. Go to page properties, but instead of *Test*, mark this page as a *Suite*.

Copy the common code (namespace import, test environment set-up and the player registration) and paste it into the contents of a new page called *PurchaseTicketSuite.SetUp*. *SetUp* is a special page, and is included automatically at the beginning of all test pages in the test suite. Do not mark this page as a test.

For full code, see PurchaseTicketSuite.SetUp on page 208

```
1    !|import|
2    |Tristan.Test.PurchaseTicket|
3
4    |Set Up Test Environment|
5    |Create Draw|
6    |01/01/2008|
7
8    |Player Registers|
9    |username|password|name|address|city|postcode|country|new player id?|
10   |john|test123|John Smith|44 Ranelagh Way|London|NN1EE1|UK|>>player|
```

Then take the rest of the test pages, which describe actual business rules, from section *"Writing the story in a test table"* on page 62 and section *"Use DoFixture keywords for better control"* on page 66 and put them in separate pages below *PurchaseTicketSuite*. Call the first something like *BasicCase*, and the second *NotEnoughMoney*. Mark them both as tests. Once the pages are marked as tests, *SetUp* is automatically included into them (Figure 7.1).

Figure 7.1. SetUp is automatically included in all tests in a test suite

When you look at the *PurchaseTicketSuite* page now, it should list three child pages and have a *Suite* button on the left. Click **Suite** to run all the tests in the suite. The page starts with a test summary, followed by individual test reports (Figure 7.2).

Figure 7.2. Fitnesse shows a summary at the beginning of the test suite report

In what order are suite pages executed?

The order of pages is not guaranteed, so do not depend on it. Extract all common functionality into the *SetUp* page so that the order is not important.

While refactoring your test pages to extract common things to a SetUp page, be careful not to lose the expressiveness of the page. The important thing is that everyone has the same understanding of what the test page describes — so do not make the page too technical.

Include pages and use them as components

You can create as many levels of subwiki hierarchies as you like: sublevels automatically inherit the parent *SetUp* pages. However, once you create a *SetUp* page in a subwiki, the parent *SetUp* is no longer called automatically. To execute the parent *SetUp* page, include it in the subwiki *SetUp* with an !include directive, followed by the page name.

We can also use this trick to include other pages. This allows us to create a set of utility fixtures (such as register customer, process order) and use them as components in other tests.

If the output of utility tables is not important for the particular test, consider putting them in a collapsed block using !include -c. A collapsed block is hidden by default, so it saves some screen space.

How do I hide SetUp and TearDown?

SetUp and *TearDown* are included automatically in test suite pages, so you cannot use the !include -c trick or !*> syntax . However, FitNesse enables us to hide these two components by defining two special markup variables:

```
!define COLLAPSE_SETUP {true}
!define COLLAPSE_TEARDOWN {true}
```

You can define these two variables in the main test suite page, and they will affect all subpages.

Links within a subwiki

A subwiki hierarchy is considered a namespace for links. So, for example, link *BasicCase* from the *PurchaseTicketSuite.SetUp* page leads directly to

PurchaseTicketSuite.BasicCase. However, the main suite page *PurchaseT-icketSuite* is not in the same namespace, but one level above. If you put a link named *BasicCase* in the main suite page, it will lead to a top-level *BasicCase* page. To reach a subpage, prefix the name with a caret (*^Basic-Case*). In FitNesse release 20070619, symbols < and > are also used to point one level up or down in the hierarchy. To go to the top level, prefix a page name with a dot. So the link to *.FrontPage* always leads to the home page of the site. This is a good candidate to put in the common page footer (see section *"Defining common actions"* on page 77).

Reuse entire suites with symbolic links

FitNesse tables do not specify the code implementation, just the class and method names for the fixtures. We can reuse the whole test suite with a different set-up to verify two different implementations of the same interface. For example, we can use the same tables to check a web service layer and a local implementation by importing a different names-pace.

Including individual pages is not effective in this case, because we have to remember to include new pages when they are created. A better approach is to use *symbolic links*, which are effectively aliases for exist-ing pages. To include entire test suites, create a top-level page with a different set-up, and then open properties for this page. In the *Symbolic Links* section, enter the link label in the *Page Name* field and enter the destination page reference[2] in the *Path To Page* field. It is best to use ! contents -R to build the contents for the top-level page, so there's no need to worry about listing individual links.

This approach is also very effective when you want to run the same test suite against several environments, for example, two databases.

Use markup variables to parameterise test pages

In addition to symbols (described in section *"Use symbols to pass dynamic information"* on page 49), FitNesse supports simpler parameters called *markup variables*. Markup variables are similar to preprocessing macros, and we can use them to parameterise a test page (or a set of pages). For example, if the tests depend on a file system path or URL of some internal test server, which can change in the future, we can store this URL

---

[2] Page reference syntax is explained in section *"Links within a subwiki"* on page 74

in a markup variable. When the URL changes, we just need to modify it in one place.

We can specify markup variables with the !define directive. You have already used variables to specify the test runner and DLL path. Once defined, variables can be used anywhere in the wiki page by enclosing the variable name in ${}. Here is an example that shows how a variable might be used in the PurchaseTicket test:

For full code, see PurchaseTicketWithVariable on page 209

```
5   !define username {john}
19  |Purchase Ticket|
20  |Player|${username}|Deposits|100|dollars with card|4111111111111111|and
expiry date|01/12|
21  |Player|${username}|has|100|dollars|
22  |Player|${username}|buys a ticket with numbers|1,3,4,5,8,10| for |10|
dollars for draw on |01/01/2008|
```

You can use markup variables in combination with the !include directive to parameterise included pages. You can even include the same page several times, changing variable values in between. See http://fitnesse.org/FitNesse.ParameterizedIncludes for an example.

What is the difference between variables and symbols?

Markup variables are processed by the wiki, before running tests. Symbols are processed by the FIT engine while running tests. Because of that, variables can be used even as a part of cell content. This will not work:

```
|StringFixture|
|field|field?|
|acrobat <<reader|acrobat reader|
```

but you can use a markup variable:

```
|StringFixture|
|field|field?|
|acrobat ${reader}|acrobat reader|
```

Symbols are also available to fixtures at runtime, and variables are not.

Defining common actions

In addition to *SetUp*, you can also create a *TearDown* page that will be executed after each test. *SuiteSetUp* and *SuiteTearDown* pages, if they exist, are executed when the entire suite starts and ends respectively. You can define common content that is not test related with *PageHeader* and *PageFooter* special pages in each subwiki. The suite page can also contain common path definitions. In addition, there is a special *root* page that defines global definitions for the entire system. So there are quite a few options for defining common content for several pages. Here are a few simple guidelines on what to use and when:

- Put common HTML content like documentation links into *PageHeader* and *PageFooter*, as they are pasted directly into the page code. *SetUp* and *TearDown* are not good for this because they will have a border when displayed on screen.
- If you use FitNesse only for .NET testing, add global path and runner definitions for including basic FIT libraries and setting up a .NET 2 runner to */root*.
- Put project-specific DLL paths in the main test suite page. FitNesse looks for path definitions up the hierarchy, so this ensures that correct DLLs will be loaded for all the tests.
- Put package includes and initialisations such as the setup of a database connection pool in either *SuiteSetUp* or *SetUp*. The difference is that *SetUp* is executed before each test, and *SuiteSetUp* is executed once only for the entire test suite. Also, in FitNesse releases before 20070619 *SuiteSetUp* does not run when you execute individual test pages from a suite.
- Add actions that have to be executed once and only once for the entire suite run to *SuiteSetUp*.
- Extract utility tables that perform common processing or tests into pages outside the test hierarchy, and then include them in tests with the `!include` directive.

Remove irrelevant information

We reused a registration table from Chapter 5, *Writing simple test scripts*, to create a new player for tests in this chapter. Although every programmer knows that it is nice to reuse existing code, watch out for this kind of reuse, especially when you copy several tables from another page just to set the stage for a new test.

As the project advances, you often add new tests as extensions of previous tests, continuing a bigger story or checking an alternative scenario. In these cases, you might just copy parts of existing pages or even complete pages into the new setup. Chances are that these new tests don't need that much detail. Having five large tables up front that check irrelevant conditions, just to prepare the stage for another test, only makes the pages harder to read and maintain.

Treat your test pages like code. When you see duplication, refactor it. Having copies of groups of tables in various pages, or used together to set up tests, is a good signal that they should be consolidated into a smaller utility table. It might also be a signal that you are not testing the business rules directly.

> ### Don't test workflow, get to business rules
>
> Having a lot of similar tests might signal that you are focusing too much on the workflow, not on the underlying rules. This is, in most cases, a waste of time. Rick Mugridge[3] warns that you can easily get disillusioned with automated testing if you write a lot of workflow tests, because they will be a pain to maintain. Rick suggests that maintenance problems are a sign that business rules are not being expressed directly. Looking for the common features of the tests and cutting to the essentials is a way to reduce significantly the effort of writing and maintaining tests. It also makes clearer any parts of business rules that are not being tested.

All the user details in this chapter are unimportant. The full registration table is relevant only for the original test, where we had to verify that correct data is stored in the system. All we want to do in this case is to create a new user called John. We can write a new fixture that quickly creates a new user and use this instead of the big table in tests from this chapter. Because we are not interested in user details, we can just randomly create user properties.

Acceptance tests should focus on business rules

We can even go a bit further and throw out deposits from ticket purchase tests. In the tests in this chapter, depositing money is not really part of

---

[3] see page 133 of *Fit for Developing Software*[2]

the relevant business rule. This step is just a utility to get some money into the account, so that we can check actual business rules. If the new utility fixture pays some money directly into the account after creating the player, then we can delete the deposit step, and skip the payment provider and mock object issue completely.

As a project evolves, you might often notice that parts of tests can be thrown out without any loss of the meaning. When the problem domain becomes clearer and after refactoring exercises that clean up the design, check whether some parts of tests can be removed to make them more focused on business rules.

Hide parts of the page

Sometimes you can make test pages easier to read by hiding unimportant parts. To mark part of the page as a collapsible block, put a line containing !* and the section name before the start of a block, and a line containing *! after the end of the block. People viewing the page can then hide the block by clicking its name. If you start the block with !*> it is automatically hidden. Here is an example:

```
!* Block 1
This block is collapsible, but open by default
*!

!*> Block 2
This block is collapsible, but hidden by default
*!
```

Playtime

Here is some stuff to try on your own:

- Define the username as a variable in the *SetUp* page and replace all occurrences of John in test pages with this variable. Change the variable value to Arthur and see whether tests still pass.

Stuff to remember

- `!contents -R` automatically builds a table of contents for a test suite.
- `!include` embeds the contents of another page.
- Symbolic links are page aliases, and you can use them to import entire suites.
- Markup variables are preprocessing macros that you can use to replace parts of cell contents.
- You can group related tests into test suites to remove duplication.
- Tests evolve during a project, and like code, they need occasional housekeeping. Watch out for duplication and irrelevant content.

Chapter 8.

Coordinating fixtures

In Chapter 6, *Writing efficient test scripts*, we saw how we can write tests almost in plain English with DoFixture. However, for some test steps it is better to use a more compact format, especially when actions or data have a repetitive structure. Luckily, we can mix and match with DoFixture: use story-like rows when this makes sense, and use other fixtures when we need a more compact structure. Let's see how DoFixture can embed other fixtures.

In this chapter, we'll implement the following user story:

Pay out winnings

As an operator, I want the system to find winning tickets, calculate winnings and pay money into ticket holders' accounts when I enter draw results.

Just as with previous stories, our first concern is how to test that the system works as expected. Our business analysts come up with a few ideas:

- Let's put four tickets in a draw, each worth 50 dollars, for completely different numbers. Then let's enter draw results that match all six numbers on one of the tickets. Other tickets do not match any drawn numbers. The owner of the winning ticket should take 68% of the payout pool. The total pool value is 200 dollars and the operator takes 50%, which leaves 100 for prizes. The prize for six winning numbers is 68 dollars. So the owner of this ticket should have 18 dollars more than he had before (68 in prize money minus 50 paid for the ticket). The other three players should have 50 dollars less than they started with.

- Let's register four tickets as before, but have two tickets with four common numbers, and then draw these numbers along with two others not appearing on any ticket. The owners of two winning tickets should split 10% of the payout pool in proportion to their ticket values. To test the proportional split, let's have one ticket at 80 dollars and the other at 20 dollars, so the prize should be split 4/1.

The first thing that these tests signal is that tickets can have different values. Luckily, our ITicket interface already provides this, so we don't have to refactor. Also, the test scripts hint that some parts of the tests need a story-based structure (draw results) and other parts need a repetitive structure (buy multiple tickets, check winnings for each ticket). So we have to combine what we learned in the previous two chapters.

Embed fixtures for best results

DoFixture allows us to embed other fixtures into tests. To embed fixtures, we first need to split one big table into several smaller ones. DoFixture allows this with a feature called *flow*: if the first test class on a page is a subclass of DoFixture, it takes over the whole page, and allows us to split the rows into individual tables.

When the page is in flow mode, the test rows are first matched to flow fixture methods. If no corresponding method exists, then a fixture is created normally, taking the class name from the first row. So, we can keep using tables for test steps where needed. If a method of a flow test returns a Fixture instance, the rest of the current table is then analysed as if it was specified for this fixture. So we can use a DoFixture method to prepare a ColumnFixture for execution. In flow mode we can embed and reuse fixtures without depending on them to read the context. This is the FitNesse version of *dependency injection,*[1] which makes writing and combining fixtures much easier.

Flow scripts are much easier to read, as the first row of a table does not have to be devoted to specifying the class name. Also, flow mode allows us to define and store the context of a test script in private variables of a test fixture, rather than static global variables.

Settlement tests in flow mode

We'll use a DoFixture in flow mode for the settlement test script. This fixture provides context to other fixtures. We'll need to give other fixtures a reference to a player manager and a draw manager, so that they can work on the same accounts and tickets. In addition, we'll need to open a draw in order to register tickets. Because draw details are not really important for this test, let's just create a draw in the background, without requiring anything to be done explicitly in the test. This is

---

[1] A software pattern in which service references and configuration are passed to the object by the framework, without any code in the object to request or locate the services and configuration. This pattern leads to loose coupling and objects that are much easier to test and combine. Objects using this pattern also have less code because they are not responsible for reaching out to services or reading the configuration.

an example of simplifying tests as explained in section *"Remove irrelevant information"* on page 77. Our flow fixture initialises these "service objects" and other fixtures use them later:

For full code, see Tristan/test/Settlement.cs on page 196

```
62    public class SettlementTest:DoFixture
63    {
64        private IDrawManager drawManager;
65        private IPlayerManager playerManager;
66        private DateTime drawDate;
67        public SettlementTest()
68        {
69          playerManager = new PlayerManager();
70          drawManager = new DrawManager(playerManager);
71          drawDate = DateTime.Now;
72          drawManager.CreateDraw(drawDate);
73        }
90    }
```

To start a test in flow mode, create a table for the flow fixture class at the top of the page. This table typically contains just the class name. Because this must be the first table on the page, the class name must be fully qualified (with the namespace). We cannot even use the import directive before a flow table.

For full code, see SettlementTests.SetUp on page 210

```
1    !|Tristan.Test.Settlement.SettlementTest|
```

If this first table, which just holds the test name, starts confusing your non-technical users or customers, put a short test description after the initial setup (use !3 before it to create a third-level heading). Then tell customers to ignore everything above the heading and focus on the part below the title.

Use SetUpFixture to prepare the stage for tests

Next, let's create four players to buy tickets. Although player details are not relevant for the test, having named players makes it easier to verify test results. Since we want to check the player balances at the end, explicitly specifying the starting balances also makes results easier to verify. Ideally, we would like to use a table with player name and initial balance, and hide all other properties:

For full code, see SettlementTests.SetUp on page 210

```
3    |Accounts before the draw|
4    |player|balance|
5    |Arthur|100|
6    |Ford|100|
7    |Trisha|100|
8    |Marvin|100|
```

We could use a column fixture with two fields and a create method to set up the players. However, there is a better solution called SetUpFixture.

SetUpFixture is another one of Rick Mugridge's classes from FitLibrary. It is a good replacement for ColumnFixture when we just want to prepare data, not to test anything. Instead of populating ColumnFixture properties and then calling a method to create a player, SetUpFixture requires us to implement just one method, and does not have the additional utility column on the screen. Join column headers to get the method name (the trick from tip *"Don't type method names, copy them"* on page 64 also works on SetUpFixture), and declare method parameters to match column values. Here is a quick way to create a player and assign an initial balance:

For full code, see Tristan/test/Settlement.cs on page 196

```
26    internal class CreatePlayerFixture : SetUpFixture
27    {
28      private IPlayerManager _playerManager;
29      public CreatePlayerFixture(IPlayerManager pm)
30      {
31        _playerManager = pm;
32      }
33      public void PlayerBalance(String player, decimal balance)
34      {
35        PlayerRegistrationInfo p = new PlayerRegistrationInfo();
36        p.Username = player; p.Name = player;
37        p.Password = "XXXXXX";
38        // define other mandatory properties
39        int playerId = _playerManager.RegisterPlayer(p);
40        _playerManager.AdjustBalance(playerId, balance);
41      }
42    }
```

Method PlayerBalance is used to execute our table rows, because the table has two columns: player and balance. We now need to connect this

fixture to prepared service objects. We do this in a new method in our
SettlementTest. The method is named AccountsBeforeTheDraw, because our
business analysts named the intial table "Accounts before the draw":

For full code, see Tristan/test/Settlement.cs on page 196

```
86      public Fixture AccountsBeforeTheDraw()
87      {
88        return new CreatePlayerFixture(playerManager);
89      }
```

The first row in the test table does not specify a fixture class name, but
a method of the DoFixture instance in flow mode. This gives us more
freedom over fixture class names. They no longer have to be customer-
friendly, because customers never see the class names of utility fixtures
directly. All rows after the first are used just as if they were part of a
normal SetUpFixture table.

Next, we need to put some tickets into the draw. Again, let's use an
embedded SetUpFixture. We are not concerned with exact draw details,
so let's hide the draw completely from the test tables and pass it directly
from the enclosing DoFixture. This leaves us with player name, selected
numbers and the ticket value for the ticket table.

For full code, see SettlementTests.OneWinnerSixBallsFirstTry on page 210

```
3    |Tickets in the Draw|
4    |player|numbers|value|
5    |Ford|2,11,22,33,39,18|50|
6    |Arthur|1,5,4,7,9,20|50|
7    |Trisha|10,21,30,6,16,26|50|
8    |Marvin|12,13,14,15,16,17|50|
```

FIT calls the PlayerNumbersValue method for each row of the table:

For full code, see Tristan/test/Settlement.cs on page 196

```
43     internal class TicketPurchaseFixture: SetUpFixture
44     {
45       private IDrawManager _drawManager;
46       private DateTime _drawDate;
47       private IPlayerManager _playerManager;
48
49       public TicketPurchaseFixture(IPlayerManager pm, IDrawManager dm,
```

```
50          DateTime drawDate)
51      {
52          _drawManager = dm;
53          _playerManager = pm;
54          _drawDate = drawDate;
55      }
56      public void PlayerNumbersValue(String player, int[] numbers, decimal
  value)
57      {
58          _drawManager.PurchaseTicket(_drawDate,
59              _playerManager.GetPlayer(player).PlayerId, numbers, value);
60      }
61  }
```

To initialise this fixture, let's add a TicketsInTheDraw method to Settle-mentTest:

For full code, see Tristan/test/Settlement.cs on page 196

```
74      public Fixture TicketsInTheDraw()
75      {
76          return new TicketPurchaseFixture(playerManager, drawManager,
  drawDate);
77      }
```

The next step is to enter draw results and settle the draw.

For full code, see SettlementTests.OneWinnerSixBallsFirstTry on page 210

```
10  |Draw results are|1,5,4,20,9,7|
```

In this case there is no embedded fixture: we process the test step in a single method of SettlementTest. Again, we use the automatic conversion from a comma-separated value list to a .NET array:

For full code, see Tristan/test/Settlement.cs on page 196

```
78      public void DrawResultsAre(int[] numbers)
79      {
80          drawManager.SettleDraw(drawDate, numbers);
81      }
```

To complete our test script, we have to verify player account balances. We can use a ColumnFixture for this:

For full code, see SettlementTests.OneWinnerSixBallsFirstTry on page 210

```
12   |Accounts after the Draw|
13   |Player|Balance?|
14   |Arthur|118|
15   |Ford|50|
16   |Trisha|50|
17   |Marvin|50|
```

The embedded `ColumnFixture` is relatively simple:

For full code, see Tristan/test/Settlement.cs on page 196

```
10   internal class BalanceCheckFixture : ColumnFixture
11   {
12     private IPlayerManager _playerManager;
13     public BalanceCheckFixture(IPlayerManager pm)
14     {
15       _playerManager = pm;
16     }
17     public String player;
18     public decimal Balance
19     {
20       get
21       {
22         return _playerManager.GetPlayer(player).Balance;
23       }
24     }
25   }
```

`SettlementTest` initialises this new class just as it does other embedded fixtures:

For full code, see Tristan/test/Settlement.cs on page 196

```
82   public Fixture AccountsAfterTheDraw()
83   {
84     return new BalanceCheckFixture(playerManager);
85   }
```

The end result is shown in Figure 8.1. `SettlementTest` controls the whole page, but individual methods return embedded fixtures enabling us to benefit from the features of `DoFixture` and other fixtures.

Figure 8.1. DoFixture allows us to embed other fixtures

Can I use flow mode without weird method names?

SequenceFixture from FitLibrary allows you to use most DoFixture features, such as flow control, embedding other fixtures and wrapping business objects (see section *"Wrapping business objects with DoFixture"* on page 90), but uses a different convention for method calls: the first cell of a row is used for the method name, and all other cells define parameters. So using SequenceFixture makes more sense for functional regression tests, where you don't care much about how pages look.

Create test suites in flow mode

The second test in this chapter has two winners splitting the 4-out-of-6 prize. It follows the same basic script, with some different parameters. Let's make Arthur and Trisha guess four balls correctly (1,5,4,20). Arthur bets 80 dollars, Trisha bets 20, so the prize is split 4/1. The 4-out-of-6 prize is 10% of the payout pool (see Chapter 4, *Writing basic tests*), so Arthur should win 8 dollars, Trisha should win 2. If we use the same initial setup (giving each player 100 dollars up front), Arthur ends up with 100 (initial) - 80 (bet) + 8 (winnings)= 28 dollars. Trisha ends up with 100-20+2=82.

The initial setup is the same, so we don't want it in two places. Even though *SetUp* and *TearDown* (see section *"Group related tests into test suites"* on page 71) are separate pages in FitNesse, they are included in the body of test pages before the test runs. If we start the flow mode in *SetUp*, it will affect the entire test. We can split a flow script into several components. Let's delete the first two tables from the previous test, and put them in a common setup:

For full code, see SettlementTests.SetUp on page 210

```
1    !|Tristan.Test.Settlement.SettlementTest|
2
3    |Accounts before the draw|
4    |player|balance|
5    |Arthur|100|
6    |Ford|100|
7    |Trisha|100|
8    |Marvin|100|
```

This now allows us to write the second test more easily: we specify just tickets, results and expected account balances.

For full code, see SettlementTests.TwoWinnersFourBalls on page 210

```
1    !3 Arthur and Trisha guess 4 balls correctly (1,5,4,20). Arthur bet 80
     dollars, Trisha bet 20, so the prize is split 4/1
2
3    |Tickets in the Draw|
4    |player|numbers|value|
5    |Ford|2,11,22,33,39,18|50|
6    |Arthur|1,5,4,7,9,20|80|
7    |Trisha|10,1,20,5,4,11|20|
8    |Marvin|12,13,14,15,16,17|50|
9
10   |Draw results are|1,5,4,20,38,37|
11
12   |Accounts after the Draw|
13   |Player|Balance?|
14   |Arthur|28|
15   |Ford|50|
16   |Trisha|82|
17   |Marvin|50|
```

Wrapping business objects with DoFixture

DoFixture can wrap business objects and expose their methods and properties directly to test tables. This feature is similar to the target object of basic fixtures, but more powerful. In FitLibrary, the wrapped object is called *System under test*, and is defined by setting the protected mySystemUnderTest property.

Unlike the target object of a ColumnFixture (see section *"Use data-transfer objects directly"* on page 52), a system under test is not required to take over all responsibility for the test, so you do not have to put testing methods into data transfer objects. Even when a system under test is defined, test table rows can be mapped to enclosing DoFixture methods, so you can mix and match. Here is a DoFixture that exposes an internal Queue object, and adds a method to generate messages:

```
public class MessageLog:fitlibrary.DoFixture {
  Queue<string> queue=new Queue<string>();
  public MessageLog() {
    mySystemUnderTest=queue;
  }
  public void GenerateMessages(int count) {
    for (int i = 0; i < count; i++)
      queue.Enqueue("M" + i);
  }
}
```

We can now call methods of the embedded queue directly, and use DoFixture keywords (see section *"Use DoFixture keywords for better control"* on page 66) to check and control public properties. In the following table we access methods Enqueue and Dequeue and the Count property of the Queue class directly, without explicitly wrapping them into fixture methods.

```
!|MessageLog|
|Enqueue|directly to the queue|
|check|count|1|
|Generate|12|Messages|
|check|count|13|
|check|dequeue|directly to the queue|
```

This feature is very useful for functional tests, but is not so well suited to customer-oriented story tests.

Playtime

Here's some stuff to try on your own:

- Add a table to verify expected winnings to the tests in this chapter (hint: modify the table from Chapter 4, *Writing basic tests* and embed it into the SettlementTest).

Stuff to remember

- If DoFixture is the first table on the page, it takes over page processing (flow mode), and allows rows to be separated into different tables.
- DoFixture in flow mode can embed other fixtures for easier testing and better re-use. Just return the Fixture from a test method and then use the rest of the current table as if it described a test for this fixture.
- In flow mode, DoFixture can initialise embedded fixtures, allowing you to use private instance variables for test script context instead of global static variables.
- SetUpFixture is cleaner than ColumnFixture for preparing test data.
- To write test scripts in flow mode, put the common part of the test script into a *SetUp* page.
- A flow mode test must begin with the flow fixture class name. Not even import can be used before the test class name in flow mode.

Chapter 9.

Working with collections

Testing lists of objects is usually a pain, but FitNesse makes it very easy. So far, we have always been testing a predefined number of items or steps. Now we'll learn how to verify a bunch of objects at once using ArrayFixture and RowFixture.

In this chapter, we'll implement the following user story:

> **View tickets**
>
> As a player, I want to view my tickets, so that I can find out if I have won and how much.

The customers tell us that a player should be able to view all his open tickets (tickets for open draws) and all his tickets for any particular draw. For open draws, we need to show selected numbers, ticket value and draw date. When the player views tickets by draw, we should display selected numbers, ticket value and winnings.

Our job is done when the following test cases run correctly:

- A draw on 01/01/2008 is open, and player John has 100 dollars in his account. He buys a single ticket for numbers 1, 3, 4, 5, 8, 10; another single ticket for 2, 4, 5, 8, 10, 12; and five tickets for numbers 3, 6, 9, 12, 15, 18. When he views his open tickets, he should see three tickets for the draw on 01/01/2008, with 10 dollars on the first two sets of numbers and 50 dollars on the third set of numbers.

- Two players have tickets in the same draw. Tom buys a ticket with numbers 2, 4, 5, 8, 10, 12 for the draw on 01/01/2008. John buys a ticket with numbers 1, 3, 4, 5, 8, 10 for the same draw. When Tom views tickets for the draw on 01/01, he should see only his ticket, not John's. Likewise for John.

- Draws on 01/01, 02/01 and 03/01 are open. Player John has 100 dollars in his account. He buys a ticket with the numbers 1, 3, 4, 5, 8,10 for the draws on 01/01 and 02/01, and five tickets with numbers 3, 6, 9, 12, 15, 18 for the draw on 01/01. When he views his tickets for the draw on 01/01, he should see 10 dollars on 1, 3, 4, 5 ,8, 10 and 50 dollars on 3, 6, 9, 12, 15, 18. For the draw on 02/01, he should see just 10 dollars on 1, 3, 4, 5, 8, 10. All tickets are open. For the draw on 03/01, he should see no tickets.

- Continuing the third test, numbers 1, 3, 4, 5, 31, 32 are drawn on 01/01/2008, and John has a winning ticket with four correct numbers. Now, when he lists tickets for the draw on 01/01, he should see that both tickets are closed, and that the 10-dollar ticket has three dollars of associated winnings (the total pool was 60 dollars, the payout pool was 30 dollars, and the 4-out-of-6 prize is 10% of this). When John lists his open tickets, he should only see the ticket for 02/01.

These test scripts give us some new ideas about the problem domain. As we learned in the previous chapter, tickets can have different values. But in this case, our clients want five tickets for 10 dollars on the same set of numbers and for the same draw to appear as one 50-dollar ticket. The test scripts also call for a new kind of test: checking the contents of a list of objects (tickets a player has in a draw).

Testing lists of objects

All four tests for this chapter use a draw on 01/01 and a player called John. So let's start the test, open the draw and create this player in a common setup page:

For full code, see TicketReviewTests.SetUp on page 211

```
1   !|Tristan.Test.ReviewTickets|
2
3   |Draw on |01/01/2008| is open|
4
5   |Player | john | opens account with | 100 | dollars|
```

The first test should look like this:

For full code, see TicketReviewTests.SeveralTicketsOneDraw on page 211

```
1   |Player|john|buys a ticket with numbers|1,3,4,5,8,10|for draw on|
01/01/2008|
2
3   |Player|john|buys a ticket with numbers|2,4,5,8,10,12|for draw on|
01/01/2008|
4
5   |Player|john|buys|5|tickets with numbers|3,6,9,12,15,18|for draw on|
01/01/2008|
6
```

```
7    |Player|john|lists open tickets|
8    |draw|numbers|value|
9    |01/01/2008|1,3,4,5,8,10|10|
10   |01/01/2008|2,4,5,8,10,12|10|
11   |01/01/2008|3,6,9,12,15,18|50|
```

To implement this test, we need to find open tickets of a particular player. Let's add a method for this to DrawManager:

For full code, see Tristan/src/IDrawManager.cs on page 176

```
22      List<ITicket> GetOpenTickets(int playerId);
```

Everything except the last table in the test looks very similar to methods and tables from the previous two chapters. The last table presents us with a new problem, because we need to check a list of elements. In section *"Embed fixtures for best results"* on page 82 we used a Column-Fixture to check several accounts at once, but the situation here is a bit different. This test can return more or less rows than expected. Implementing this test with ColumnFixture would be relatively tricky. We would need separate checks for collection size and collection contents. In the collection contents test, we would have to create a wrapper to fetch an element by some key property (assuming that there is a key property), and then test other properties. DoFixture has a very useful shortcut for tests like these: it just returns the whole list. See the method PlayerListsOpenTickets below.

For full code, see Tristan/test/ReviewTickets.cs on page 193

```
9     public class ReviewTickets:fitlibrary.DoFixture
10    {
11      private IDrawManager _drawManager;
12      private IPlayerManager _playerManager;
13      public ReviewTickets()
14      {
15        _playerManager = new PlayerManager();
16        _drawManager = new DrawManager(_playerManager);
17      }
18      public void DrawOnIsOpen(DateTime drawDate)
19      {
20        _drawManager.CreateDraw(drawDate);
21      }
22      public void PlayerOpensAccountWithDollars(String player, decimal
     balance)
23        {
```

```
24        PlayerRegistrationInfo p = new PlayerRegistrationInfo();
25        p.Username = player; p.Name = player;
26        p.Password = "XXXXXX";
27        // define other mandatory properties
28        int playerId = _playerManager.RegisterPlayer(p);
29        _playerManager.AdjustBalance(playerId, balance);
30      }
31    public void PlayerBuysATicketWithNumbersForDrawOn(
32        string username, int[] numbers, DateTime date)
33    {
34        PlayerBuysTicketsWithNumbersForDrawOn(username, 1, numbers, date);
35    }
36
37    public void PlayerBuysTicketsWithNumbersForDrawOn(
38        string username, int tickets, int[] numbers, DateTime date)
39    {
40        int pid = _playerManager.GetPlayer(username).PlayerId;
41        _drawManager.PurchaseTicket(date, pid, numbers, 10 * tickets);
42    }
43    public IList<ITicket> PlayerListsOpenTickets(String player)
44    {
45        return _drawManager.GetOpenTickets(
46          _playerManager.GetPlayer(player).PlayerId);
47    }
58  }
```

If a DoFixture method returns an array or an IEnumerable collection, the result is automatically wrapped into an ArrayFixture for testing. Array-Fixture is a FitLibrary class for testing arrays and collections. It can check contents of an array and verify that there are no additional or missing elements. The second row of an ArrayFixture table lists element properties,[1] and all the following rows contain the expected contents of the array. Properties not included in the table are just ignored when comparing actual results with expected results, so you can hide unimportant details. ArrayFixture compares the array or collection with the table by checking all the given properties, in the order of the elements listed in the table. It reports any elements out of order, elements that were not in the test method result (marked as missing), and elements returned by the test method that were not expected in the table (marked as surplus).

The first test is now complete (Figure 9.1). Now that we know how to test lists of objects, we can easily write the second and third test cases for this chapter. Let's check for the tickets using the table header "Player XXX lists tickets for draw on YYY". The second test looks like this:

---

[1] Properties in a general sense: fields and methods (without parameters) can also be used.

For full code, see TicketReviewTests.TwoAccountsOneDraw on page 212

```
1    |Player|tom|opens account with|50|dollars|
2
3    |Player|john|buys a ticket with numbers|1,3,4,5,8,10|for draw on|
01/01/2008|
4
5    |Player|tom|buys a ticket with numbers|2,4,5,8,10,12|for draw on|
01/01/2008|
6
7    |Player|john|lists tickets for draw on|01/01/2008|
8    |value|numbers|
9    |10|1,3,4,5,8,10|
10
11   |Player|tom|lists tickets for draw on|01/01/2008|
12   |value|numbers|
13   |10|2,4,5,8,10,12|
```

To implement it, we'll need a method in the main test fixture that returns a list of tickets in a draw for a player:

For full code, see Tristan/test/ReviewTickets.cs on page 193

```
48       public IList<ITicket> PlayerListsTicketsForDrawOn(
49         String player, DateTime date)
50       {
51         return _drawManager.GetTickets(
52           date,_playerManager.GetPlayer(player).PlayerId);
53       }
```

And a corresponding method in `DrawManager`:

For full code, see Tristan/src/IDrawManager.cs on page 176

```
23       List<ITicket> GetTickets(DateTime drawDate, int playerId);
```

Checking for empty collections

The third test case presents us with a new problem: the draw on 03/01 should have no tickets. Testing empty collections is similar to testing collections with elements, but the table syntax might seem a bit strange. Even for empty collections, we have to describe the structure of the element object in the second table row, but there are no element rows below it.

For full code, see TicketReviewTests.SeveralTicketsTwoDraws on page 211

```
1   |Draw on|02/01/2008|is open|
2
3   |Draw on|03/01/2008|is open|
4
5   |Player|john|buys a ticket with numbers|1,3,4,5,8,10|for draw on|
02/01/2008|
6
7   |Player|john|buys a ticket with numbers|1,3,4,5,8,10|for draw on|
01/01/2008|
8
9   |Player|john|buys|5|tickets with numbers|3,6,9,12,15,18|for draw on|
01/01/2008|
10
11  |Player|john|lists tickets for draw on|01/01/2008|
12  |value|numbers|
13  |10|1,3,4,5,8,10|
14  |50|3,6,9,12,15,18|
15
16  |Player|john|lists tickets for draw on|02/01/2008|
17  |value|numbers|
18  |10|1,3,4,5,8,10|
19
20  |Player|john|lists tickets for draw on|03/01/2008|
21  |value|numbers|
```

If the draw on 03/01 had any tickets, FitNesse would display them in the last table and fail the test.

How do I test arrays of strings or ints?

Although embedded types don't have any properties you can put into the table header, they all have a ToString method, which will do just fine for this purpose. So your table might look like this:

```
!|Some method returning array of ints |
| ToString |
| 1 |
| 2 |
| 5 |
```

Remember the exclamation mark at the beginning of the table to prevent CamelCase formatting of ToString.

Figure 9.1. DoFixture automatically wraps arrays and IEnumerable collections into ArrayFixture, allowing us to easily verify their contents.

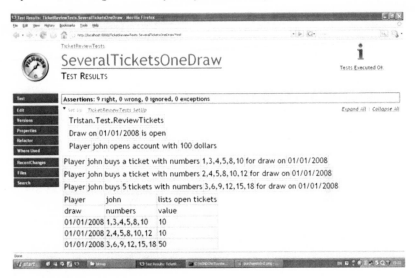

Beware of test extensions

Although the fourth test our clients requested seems like an extension of the third test, in fact all they share is a common setup. Verifications in the third test are irrelevant to the fourth one. Beware of tests that seem like extensions of some other test cases. Instead of blindly including the contents of another test page, think about extracting a common setup and focusing on the actual business rules that are being tested.

In order to check that winnings are correctly recorded against tickets, let's set up draws, enter results for the draw on 01/01, and then check the tickets.

For full code, see TicketReviewTests.WinningsRecordedCorrectly on page 212

```
1   |Draw on|02/01/2008|is open|
2
3   |Player|john|buys a ticket with numbers|1,3,4,5,8,10|for draw on|
01/01/2008|
4
5   |Player|john|buys a ticket with numbers|1,3,4,5,8,10|for draw on|
02/01/2008|
```

```
 6
 7    |Player|john|buys|5|tickets with numbers|3,6,9,12,15,18|for draw on|
01/01/2008|
 8
 9    |Numbers|1,3,4,5,31,32|are drawn on|01/01/2008|
10
11    |Player|john|lists tickets for draw on|01/01/2008|
12    |value|numbers|is open|winnings|
13    |10|1,3,4,5,8,10|false|3|
14    |50|3,6,9,12,15,18|false|0|
15
16    |Player|john|lists open tickets|
17    |draw|value|numbers|
18    |02/01/2008|10|1,3,4,5,8,10|
```

To display winnings along with tickets, we have to modify the settlement to store calculated winnings for individual tickets. Luckily we already have tests for this, developed in Chapter 8, *Coordinating fixtures*, so we can refactor them easily.

The settlement process for a single draw can take a long time, so a player could theoretically view his tickets during the process. This might be a problem, because some tickets will be settled and some will still be open, but this will not be obvious to the player. To avoid inconsistencies, we'll add a new field to the ticket specifying whether or not it is open. We'll also need to add a draw date to the ticket, so that we can show it. Our ITicket interface gets these new fields:

For full code, see Tristan/src/ITicket.cs on page 178

```
12    bool IsOpen { get;}
13    decimal Winnings { get; }
14    DateTime draw { get; }
```

To complete the test code, we just need one more method in the main test fixture to enter the draw results:

For full code, see Tristan/test/ReviewTickets.cs on page 193

```
54    public void NumbersAreDrawnOn(int[] numbers, DateTime date)
55    {
56      _drawManager.SettleDraw(date, numbers);
57    }
```

Can I use a Draw object instead of DateTime?

You can use any business-domain object in FitNesse cells as long as it can be uniquely represented by a string. Define a static method Parse to convert from a string to your business class, override ToString in the class for the opposite conversion and override Equals to provide comparisons. Then, use the class just as you would use numbers or strings in FitNesse. If you want to use a system or third-party class to which you cannot add the Parse method, you can tell FitNesse how to use it by implementing a custom cell handler. See section *"Simplify verifications with a custom cell handler"* on page 158 for instructions on how to do this.

Use RowFixture for better precision

Here is a quick task for you: modify any ArrayFixture test table from this chapter to contain a wrong value, for example change the ticket value 10 to 11. The report gives you quick feedback that something is wrong, but it's not very easy to tell exactly what (Figure 9.2).

Figure 9.2. We just changed one digit, but ArrayFixture shows a lot of errors

Player	john	lists open tickets
draw	numbers	value
01/01/2008	1,3,4,5,8,10	10
01/01/2008 missing	2,4,5,8,10,12	11
01/01/2008 out of order	3,6,9,12,15,18	50
01/01/2008 00:00:00 surplus	2,4,5,8,10,12	10

There is a better solution: RowFixture is a test class from the main FIT.NET library, and is a good replacement for ArrayFixture when you want better precision.[2] Although these two classes have many similar features, RowFixture is much better at matching objects to table rows. For example, if we put a question mark after ticket value in the second row of the table, this tells FitNesse not to use this column for matching objects. FitNesse still compares the actual ticket value with the expected one, but does not complain about missing and additional objects. As you can see in Figure 9.3, the problem is much easier to spot than in Figure 9.2.

---

[2] Actually, ArrayFixture was built as a replacement for RowFixture, and is used perhaps more often today because of its tight integration with DoFixture.

Figure 9.3. A single wrong value can be spotted much easier with RowFixture

Player	john	lists open tickets
draw	numbers	value?
01/01/2008	1,3,4,5,8,10	10
		11 *expected*
01/01/2008	2,4,5,8,10,12	
		10 *actual*
01/01/2008	3,6,9,12,15,18	50

RowFixture allows us to split the properties into properties that define an identity (equivalent to a database primary key), and auxiliary values that are not used to decide whether an object appears in the results or not. Just put a question mark after each auxiliary value in the table header. It is good practice to keep identity columns on the left and auxiliary values on the right, because RowFixture can get confused when these columns are mixed in some versions of FIT.NET.

So, we can replace the ArrayFixture with a RowFixture and get better error reports. DoFixture does not wrap an array automatically into a RowFixture, so we'll have to do a bit of work ourselves. The new test table can also be embedded into the main DoFixture, in a similar way to the ColumnFixture example in Chapter 8, *Coordinating fixtures*. RowFixture is an abstract class, so we have to override two methods to implement it:

```
public override Type GetTargetClass()
public override object[] Query()
```

GetTargetClass is used to map table columns to properties and should return the collection element type (in this case, ITicket). Query should return the array of elements we want to test. So let's write a generic RowFixture that wraps ITicket lists:

For full code, see Tristan/test/ReviewTickets.cs on page 193

```
112    public class TicketRowFixture : fit.RowFixture
113    {
114      private List<ITicket> _internalList;
115      public TicketRowFixture(List<ITicket> tickets)
116      {
117        _internalList = tickets;
118      }
119      public override Type GetTargetClass()
120      {
121        return typeof(ITicket);
122      }
123
```

```
124    public override object[] Query()
125    {
126      return _internalList.ToArray();
127    }
128  }
```

We'll use this class instead of directly returning a list from the main fixture class:

For full code, see Tristan/test/ReviewTickets.cs on page 193

```
94     public RowFixture PlayerListsOpenTickets(String player)
95     {
96       return new TicketRowFixture(
97         _drawManager.GetOpenTickets(
98           _playerManager.GetPlayer(player).PlayerId));
99     }
100    public RowFixture PlayerListsTicketsForDrawOn(
101      String player, DateTime date)
102    {
103      return new TicketRowFixture(
104        _drawManager.GetTickets(date,
105          _playerManager.GetPlayer(player).PlayerId));
106    }
```

As RowFixture is part of the basic Fit library, it uses FIT cell handlers (see section *"Cell operation handlers"* on page 154). Rather like ActionFixture, explained in section *"Keep ActionFixture in mind"* on page 67, this enables us to use keywords and symbols and check for detailed errors. ArrayFixture does not allow this. We can even use yes and no with RowFixture to make the test page easier to read instead of true and false.

Another important difference is that RowFixture ignores the order of elements, while ArrayFixture expects the objects to appear in the same order as in the table. FitLibrary also has a SetFixture, which is automatically used to wrap Set collections. SetFixture also ignores the order of elements.

Can I use RowFixture when element order is important?

Yes. A common trick is to add a field to the data class, specifying the index of an element in the array. This element is then listed in the table, and is typically used for row-key mapping (all other columns would have a question mark in this case).

Playtime

Here's some stuff to try on your own:

- Change the test class in this chapter to re-use `CreatePlayerFixture` from Chapter 8, *Coordinating fixtures*, to open accounts.
- Revisit the tests in Chapter 6, *Writing efficient test scripts*, and check the actual tickets, not just the number of tickets in a draw

Stuff to remember

- You can use `ArrayFixture` from FitLibrary and `RowFixture` from the basic FIT package to test lists of elements.
- If a `DoFixture` method returns an array or an `IEnumerable` collection, the result is automatically wrapped into an `ArrayFixture` for testing.
- `RowFixture` can use symbols, keywords and partial row-key mapping, so it is better then `ArrayFixture` when you need more precision.
- `ArrayFixture` checks for missing and additional elements.
- You must specify element structure (second row) even when checking for an empty collection.
- Columns with a question mark in `RowFixture` are excluded from the "primary key".

Part III. Advanced FitNesse usage

Now that you've mastered basic FitNesse skills, it's time to learn how FitNesse cooperates with other tools in a typical software project ecosystem.

In this part we look at how to set up FitNesse for a team of developers and how to utilise it for testing web and database code. We also review some nice FitNesse features that help with legacy code maintenance.

Finally, we dive deeper into the heart of FIT to see how things really work, and how we can customise FIT and FitNesse to particular project needs.

Chapter 10.

Working in a team

One of the best features of FitNesse is that it promotes a collaborative way of working. Now is the time to learn how to set up and use FitNesse in a team environment. In this chapter we also consider various options for server deployment and configuration and discuss how to integrate FitNesse with automated build tools and build servers.

Options for team setup

There is no general agreement on how best to use FitNesse as a team tool so we review pros and cons for the three most popular options rather than suggest a one-size-fits-all solution.

- Using a single central server
- Importing tests from a remote wiki
- Storing tests in a version control system

Choose the one that fits your team the best.

Using a single central server

In view of the fact that FitNesse works like a web server, it's only natural to think about setting up a single central test server so that team members can use the server from any machine in the network with a browser.

Technically, a single FitNesse server is capable of supporting a multi-user environment. FitNesse has an internal version control system that keeps track of test revisions, and it automatically saves a backup when pages change. Old versions are archived into ZIP files. It can also track and authenticate named users.[1] However, FitNesse cannot automatically pull files from an external repository[2] or compile them. So, if you want a central test system, you will probably want to set up a periodic build on

---

[1] see http://fitnesse.org/FitNesse.PasswordFile
[2] This feature was in development while this book was being prepared. As of release 20070619, this feature was still not in the main branch. See http://msmvps.com/blogs/jon.skeet/archive/2006/02/14/fitnessesvn.aspx and http://www.yoda.arachsys.com/java/fitnesse/ for some workarounds.

the same machine, so that the latest code is always available for testing. Because tests are executed using an external program, no object code is cached and you just need to update the DLLs for tests to pick up the latest version of your code.

How secure is FitNesse?

I find that it is easier to secure FitNesse at the firewall or load balancer level than at the application level. FitNesse is not a high-load general-purpose web server: it is a specialised web server intended to help people to write tests more easily in a collaborative environment. So I recommend that you do not count too much on the service itself providing top-notch security.

Although this setup might seem like the natural choice, in practice it works only for small teams. FitNesse does not perform well when people are running tests simultaneously. It was designed to make test management easier, not to be a scalable and robust general-purpose web server. If the central system has a separate build process then developers have to commit incomplete or untested code into the main branch for the server to see it. Another option would be to allow developers to upload their DLLs to the test server, but this is only practical for the smallest teams. Even with only three or four people uploading DLLs, there can be a lot of problems due to version conflicts.

Importing tests from a remote wiki

Another option is to use one central server for collaboration but execute tests on local FitNesse installations on developer machines. The central server coordinates updates and allows FitNesse on developer machines to take the latest test scripts using a *wiki import*. Tests are never executed on the central server, so there are no issues with server code builds nor with concurrent test runs. Developers can import test pages to a local server. Instead of one **Edit** button on the left, FitNesse shows two buttons for imported pages: **Edit Locally** and **Edit Remotely**. These two buttons enable developers to update a test script just on their machine or globally.

To import tests from a remote wiki you first create the page to serve as a root for the import hierarchy (putting !contents -R as the page content might be a good idea; see section *"Group related tests into test suites"* on page 71). Then go to page properties and enter the remote wiki URL in the URL field in the "Import Wiki" section. You can import an entire hierarchy or any sublevel (just point to the correct subwiki URL). For more details of this feature, see http://fitnesse.org/FitNesse.WikiImport.

This approach requires an identical setup for local FitNesse servers on all developer systems, in order to avoid problems with different disk paths to DLLs on various machines.

Since different version control systems are used for the test scripts (central FitNesse server) and project code, occasionally there are version conflicts between code and tests if several people are working on the same modules at the same time. So developers should edit the test scripts locally and then, when all code changes are complete, send the updates to the central server. In practice, local test updates often do not find their way back to the central server. However, with a bit of discipline, this can be a good setup for a smaller team.

Storing tests in a version control system

Since most team projects use a version control system for code anyway, another common approach is to use the version control repository for storing tests instead of the central server. Test files (and often the entire FitNesse server setup) are stored in the main version control system, along with the source code. Developers start FitNesse from the local copy of the repository, and run tests locally on their machines.

The benefit of this method is that there is no conflict between code and test script versions. Everything is in the same repository. When the project folder is committed to the version control system, test scripts are committed too. Test scripts are plain text files, so modern version control systems can merge most concurrent changes correctly. This also makes maintenance easier, because there is just one code repository to back up. Finally, because the FitNesse server is also included in the repository, relative paths to project DLLs are always the same. These issues may not be important for a smaller team, but make a huge difference for larger teams.

The downside of this method is that the internal version control system in FitNesse starts getting in the way. Automatic archiving just causes headaches by polluting the version control with hundreds of ZIP files. Some very useful FitNesse functions like test refactoring simply cannot be used in a folder-based system like CVS or Subversion. FitNesse deletes and moves complete test folders during refactoring, including hidden

.cvs and .svn files, which completely confuses folder-based version control systems.

Also, not having a central server leaves people like business analysts and customers outside the loop, because they typically do not have tools to access the version control system (or cannot be bothered to start FitNesse locally on their machines). This can be solved with an additional "central" test server for people who cannot run FitNesse on their machines. The central server is not used for wiki imports, but acts as a documentation reference. It can also be used by the continuous integration server to verify the build (see sidebar *"Continuous integration"* on page 116).

In any case, if tests are kept in an external version control repository, you should turn off internal archiving by adding -e 0 to the command used for starting FitNesse. To avoid lots of reports about conflicting changes, it is also a good idea to exclude ErrorLogs and RecentChanges directories (in the wiki) from version control.

If you use a central server backed by an external version control system, it is a good idea to restart FitNesse after tests are updated. Although the DLL code is not cached, FitNesse caches test scripts and other page content. Unless the server is restarted you might not see some updates straight away.

It might also be a good idea to configure the central server as a Windows service (see tip *"Can FitNesse start automatically with Windows?"* on page 112), so that it loads automatically and that other services can restart it when needed.

Organising the files

For development tests, it seems easiest to point FitNesse at the project DLLs directly (if you are using Visual Studio they are typically in bin \debug inside the project folder). Using absolute paths can be problematic in a team environment, because people might store the same projects in different places on their local disks. But, if you put FitNesse files and tests in the same version control repository as project code, you can use a path relative to the main FitNesse folder (the one containing run.bat). This allows all developers to run tests locally and still use the same path to reference DLLs in the project build folders.

However, if your project involves remote access or depends on reflection, it might be necessary to put your DLLs in the same folder as .NET runner (FitServer.exe). Here you have two choices: either put the test runner into your project build folder, or move the DLLs into the dotnet2 directory in the FitNesse installation. The second approach is better when your tests span multiple Visual Studio projects. You don't have to copy the DLLs manually: Visual Studio can do all the dirty work. Just add the following block to csproj project files, right before the closing Project tag:

```
<PropertyGroup>
<PostBuildEvent>copy "$(TargetPath)*" "Your FitNesse DotNet2 Folder"</
PostBuildEvent>
</PropertyGroup>
```

Replace Your FitNesse DotNet2 Folder with your dotnet2 folder path. You can use the $(SolutionDir) macro to specify a path relative to the solution folder.

Why can't FitNesse find my .NET libraries?

If everything compiles fine, but FitNesse complains about missing assemblies or libraries (a typical error would be System.Runtime. Serialization.SerializationException: Cannot find the assembly [myAssembly]), try putting all the DLLs in the folder with the .NET test runner. If you installed FIT.NET integration as suggested in section *"Setting up FitNesse"* on page 13, this is the dotnet2 directory.

Paths specified in the !path directive are just used to specify assemblies to be searched for fixtures; they are not paths for loading classes. So they are not used for creating objects with reflection or deserialisation. Assemblies in the same folder as FitServer.exe are used for creating objects with reflection or deserialisation.

Don't mix quick and slow tests

It is good practice to run as many tests as possible before committing a change to the main branch, so that potential problems get flushed out earlier rather than later.

One of the key techniques for making this principle work is to separate quick and slow tests, so that one sluggish test does not prevent a developer from running dozens of quick ones.

Can FitNesse start automatically with Windows?

If you don't mind a bit of registry editing, you can easily set up FitNesse as a system service. This enables FitNesse to run in the background and start automatically with Windows. This is probably the best way to run FitNesse on a dedicated central server.

You can use `srvany.exe` and `instsrv.exe` from the Windows resource kit to run any Java program as a service, including FitNesse. First, get the appropriate resource kit for your system from http://www.microsoft.com/windows/reskits/, install it and run **instsrv.exe FitNesse c:\reskit\srvany.exe** (replace `c:\reskit\srvany.exe` with the full path of `srvany.exe` on your system).

Then, run the registry editor (`regedit.exe`), and open the `HKEY_LOCAL_MACHINE\SYSTEM\CurrentControlSet\Services\FitNesse` key. Create a subkey called `Parameters` and enter three string values into it. The first should be named `Application` and point to `java.exe` on your system. The second should be named `AppDirectory` and point to the main FitNesse folder. The third should be named `AppParameters` and contain everything after `java.exe` in the command used to start FitNesse (`run.bat`). The registry key should look the same as on the image below:

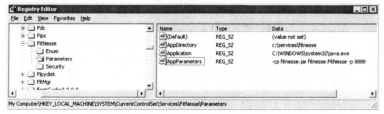

After you have done this, you can control FitNesse like any other Windows service. For more information on `srvany.exe` and a few tips on troubleshooting potential problems, see http://support.microsoft.com/kb/137890 and http://fitnesse.org/InstallingFitNesseAsaService.

What works quite well is to put fast and slow tests into different suites (or even different tools) so that they can be executed separately. This way, we run only the fast suites on every change. A build automation server runs slower tests every couple of hours and lets us know when something is broken (see section *"Scheduling tests and alerts"* on page 119).

Separate code-oriented and customer-oriented tests

FIT and FitNesse are essential tools for customer-oriented tests and validation of business rules, so acceptance tests natually sit in FitNesse. If you also use FitNesse for component or bug tests, make sure to separate customer-oriented and code-oriented groups of tests into different subwikis so that they can be executed separarately. Otherwise, customers and business analysts might start getting confused with code-related or bug-prevention tests.

Start with a fresh wiki

When you download and install FitNesse, it comes with the Java user guide, acceptance tests for the server and a lot of other things you don't really need for a .NET project, especially if you want to keep your test files in the version control system. Start with a clean slate by creating a new wiki. Just delete the FitNesseRoot directory in your FitNesse installation and restart the server: FitNesse automatically creates a new empty wiki. If you want to keep the default wiki and run your test server in parallel or on a different port, then add -r **NewWiki** to the command used to start the server (either **run.bat** or the windows service parameters). Replace NewWiki with the name of your new wiki directory.

Configure FitNesse to run .NET tests by default

By default, FitNesse runs Java tests. In section *"How FitNesse connects to .NET classes"* on page 20, we learned how to override the test runner parameters to run .NET tests. As this is a .NET testing book, it is highly probable that you will be using FitNesse mostly for .NET testing, so let's change these parameters globally. There is a special page called */root* that defines global properties. Open it for editing. (If you don't see the *Edit* button, then browse directly to */root?edit.*) Markup variables on this page are included automatically in all test suites and tests. Add the .NET test runner definitions there so that you do not have to think about this when creating individual tests and new test suites.

```
!define COMMAND_PATTERN {%m %p}
!define TEST_RUNNER {dotnet2\FitServer.exe}
!define PATH_SEPARATOR {;}
```

You can even specify paths to common DLLs with fixtures in this file so that they are automatically available for all tests. However, I think that in practice it is cleaner to keep DLL paths in test suites. When you start testing more than one DLL, it makes more sense to open a subwiki for each project and keep DLL paths in the project subwikis to avoid conflicts.

Integrating with automated build tools

Developers should run the tests and make sure that they all pass before committing code into the source code repository, so in theory the main code branch should always be stable and ready for deployment. In practice, unchecked code does get into the repository from time to time and changed dependencies cause tests and even compilations to fail. The larger the team the more often this happens. We need one more safety net to keep our code clean, something that runs all the tests without anyone pushing the button.

Automated build and integration tools can verify that the repository code can compile correctly. Luckily, FitNesse can be integrated with with such tools easily, so that tests can also be executed automatically.

Using TestRunner

When FitNesse is running as a Windows service or on a dedicated server, it is easy to integrate testing into automated build tools. In addition to FitServer.exe, which is used internally by FitNesse, the FIT.NET package contains a couple of other test runners. TestRunner.exe is intended for running tests externally, using local DLLs and a remote FitNesse server. You can find it in the dotnet2 folder in which you unpacked the FIT.NET integration.

To run a FitNesse test or suite with **TestRunner.exe**, execute the following command:

```
TestRunner.exe server port test
```

Server is the name or IP address of the machine where FitNesse is running; if you are running FitNesse on the same computer as the tests, it is localhost. Port is the port on which FitNesse is running; if you installed FitNesse as suggested in section *"Setting up FitNesse"* on page 13 this is 8888. The third argument is a test name or a test suite. For example, the following command executes the *TicketReviewTests* suite:

```
C:\services\FitNesse> dotnet2\TestRunner.exe localhost 8888
 TicketReviewTests
```

Always execute **TestRunner.exe** from the main FitNesse folder so that relative paths to DLLs in test scripts point to the same files as when running from FitNesse.

Why does TestRunner not see my DLLs?

If you start TestRunner on a remote machine, it may have problems finding DLLs from the paths specified in the FitNesse page. Double-check first that tests work OK from FitNesse. If they do, then try putting DLLs into the same folder as **TestRunner.exe**. Another option is to specify additional DLLs after the test page name, as the last argument of TestRunner (include a semi-colon on the end).

Running tests with NAnt

To run FitNesse tests from a NAnt[3] script, use the exec task to start **TestRunner.exe**. The server name and port probably won't change often, so I suggest creating a utility NAnt script that expects the test name to be passed as a parameter and has other arguments defined as local properties. Here is what the script looks like:

For full code, see scripts/runfitnesse.build on page 214

```
2   <property name="fitnesse.dir" value="c:\services\fitnesse" />
3   <property name="fitnesse.server" value="localhost" />
4   <property name="fitnesse.port" value="8888" />
5   <target name="test">
6   <exec program="${fitnesse.dir}\dotnet2\TestRunner.exe"
7   commandline="${fitnesse.server} ${fitnesse.port} ${fitnesse.test}"
8   workingdir="${fitnesse.dir}"/>
9   </target>
```

---

[3] A free build automation tool for .NET. See http://nant.sourceforge.net

Continuous integration

Continuous integration (CI) is a software development practice that requires team members to put code changes into the version control system often and try to build the whole product from source frequently, and to run tests to verify that the build is correct. Continuous integration practice leads to the holy grail of agile development: having production-quality code ready for release at almost any time. Incompatibilities between components, resurrected bugs and test failures are flushed out quickly. Because the increments are small, the problems introduced by the changes are small and they can be fixed quickly.

Early agile books, such as XP Installed[9] and the first edition of XP Explained[1], suggest having a different pair of people try the integration a few times every day and do any housekeeping required to make it run. In the last few years, a big part of the process has been automated by continuous integration servers. These tools check for source code modifications, attempt to build the whole system, run tests and warn team members about problems by email or over the web. The most popular continuous integration server for .NET is CruiseControl.NET, an open-source tool from ThoughtWorks. It even has a convenient system tray icon that uses a traffic light system to notify developers quickly that the build is failing. Microsoft has its own continuous integration solution, Team Foundation Server, which is part of the Team System version of Visual Studio. For a more detailed introduction to continuous integration, see http://www.martinfowler.com/articles/continuousIntegration.html.

Integrating FitNesse with CruiseControl.NET

It is fairly easy to integrate FitNesse with CruiseControl.NET, the most popular continuous integration server for .NET. However, there is a trick involved in formatting results. The .NET test runner does not support the XML format required by CruiseControl.NET out of the box, so we first have to run the tests and store results into a file. Then we have to format the results using the java test runner, which produces something CruiseControl.NET can read. **TestRunner.exe** has an additional option, **-results outfile.txt**, which causes it to store the output into outfile.txt. We need to execute the following two commands within CruiseControl.NET to integrate FitNesse tests:

```
C:\services\FitNesse> dotnet2\TestRunner.exe -results c:\temp
\fitnesseres.txt localhost 8888 TicketReviewTests.WinningsRecordedCorrectly
C:\services\FitNesse> java -cp fitnesse.jar fitnesse.runner.FormattingOption
c:\temp\fitnesseres.txt xml c:\temp\fitnesseres.xml localhost 8888
TicketReviewTests.WinningsRecordedCorrectly
```

Although we could use the executable[4] task from the CruiseControl.NET tasks block directly, it is better to wrap these steps into a NAnt script instead. This allows us to control whether the build should break or not (acceptance tests should typically not break the build, but unit and component tests should). Using NAnt also allows us to print some debug messages and automatically record test execution timings.

We need to create two NAnt tasks that run tests and filter results:

For full code, see scripts/runfitnesse.build on page 214

```
10   <target name="test">
11    <echo message="running tests ${fitnesse.test}" />
12    <delete file="${output.file}" />
13    <delete file="${format.file}" />
14    <exec program="${fitnesse.dir}\dotnet2\TestRunner.exe"
15    commandline="-results ${output.file} ${fitnesse.server}
  ${fitnesse.port} ${fitnesse.test}"
16    workingdir="${fitnesse.dir}"
17    failonerror="true"/>
18    <echo message="tests ${fitnesse.test} complete" />
19   </target>
20   <target name="format">
21    <echo message="formatting ${fitnesse.test} results" />
22    <delete file="${format.file}" />
23    <exec program="java.exe"
24    workingdir="${fitnesse.dir}"
25    commandline="-cp ${fitnesse.dir}\fitnesse.jar
  fitnesse.runner.FormattingOption ${output.file} xml ${format.file}
  ${fitnesse.server} ${fitnesse.port} ${fitnesse.test}" failonerror="false"/>
26    <echo message="formatting ${fitnesse.test} results into ${format.file}
  complete" />
27   </target>
```

Notice the failonerror="true" part in the first task. Set the value to false for acceptance tests, so that they do not break your build.

---

[4] http://confluence.public.thoughtworks.org/display/CCNET/Executable+Task

The first step should be executed from the tasks block and the second from the publishers block, because we want the results to be formatted even when a test fails (*even more in this case, because we want to know what went wrong*). The results can then be included into the build report in the merge[5] block. Remember to include the xmllogger publisher at the end of the publishers block,[6] to enable CruiseControl.NET to display regular build results.

FitNesse was designed to allow easy collaboration and testing, not really to be a 24/7 Internet server. At first it typically froze in our environment after a day or two of continuous testing, so we included a service restart before tests. Restarting the server also makes sure that FitNesse is using the latest versions of test scripts and not the ones cached in memory. When FitNesse is installed as a service (see tip *"Can FitNesse start automatically with Windows?"* on page 112), you can use **net.exe** to stop and re-start it. Don't use **sc.exe** because this command is asynchronous, and you definitely don't want the tests to start executing before the server is up.

Here is a complete CruiseControl.NET project configuration:

For full code, see scripts/ccnet.config on page 214

```
1   <cruisecontrol>
2   <project name="Continuous-Test">
3     <workingDirectory>w:\ccnetbuild\source\test</workingDirectory>
4     <artifactDirectory>w:\ccnetbuild\artifact-cont\test</artifactDirectory>
5     <tasks>
6     <exec>
7      <executable>net.exe</executable>
8      <buildArgs>stop ccnetfitnesse</buildArgs>
9     </exec>
10    <exec>
11     <executable>net.exe</executable>
12     <buildArgs>start ccnetfitnesse</buildArgs>
13    </exec>
14    <nant>
15       <buildFile>w:\ccnetbuild\source\build\runfitnesse.build</buildFile>

16       <buildTimeoutSeconds>300000</buildTimeoutSeconds>
17       <buildArgs>-D:output.file=c:\temp\fitnesse-tx.log -D:format.file=c:
\temp\fitnesse-tx.xml -D:fitnesse.test=TicketReviewTests</buildArgs>
```

---

[5] See http://confluence.public.thoughtworks.org/display/CCNET/File+Merge+Task for more information on result file merging.

[6] http://confluence.public.thoughtworks.org/display/CCNET/Xml+Log+Publisher

```
18    <targetList><target>test</target></targetList>
19    </nant>
20    </tasks>
21    <publishers>
22    <nant>
23      <buildFile>w:\ccnetbuild\source\build\runfitnesse.build</buildFile>

24      <buildTimeoutSeconds>300000</buildTimeoutSeconds>
25      <buildArgs>-D:output.file=c:\temp\fitnesse-tx.log -D:format.file=c:
\temp\fitnesse-tx.xml -D:fitnesse.test=TicketReviewTests</buildArgs>
26    <targetList><target>format</target></targetList>
27    </nant>
28    <merge>
29            <files>
30                    <file>c:\temp\fitnesse-tx.xml</file>
31            </files>
32        </merge>
33    <xmllogger />
34    </publishers>
35    </project>
36    </cruisecontrol>
```

If you build code and run tests in the same CruiseControl.NET project, remember to delete FitNesse results (both raw and and formatted) before the build. If you do not do this, when a build fails, the publishers block merges old FitNesse results with the failed build report. This gives a misleading report that the build failed but tests passed.

Scheduling tests and alerts

Automated build tools can signal errors and notify developers when the build fails. We can use this feature to keep track of the health of the repository code automatically. However, different types of tests call for different notifications.

Basic tests should ideally be executed on every source code change without anyone pushing the button, so it is a good idea to have these tests run as part of the basic build. This calls for basic tests to run quickly, as explained in section *"Don't mix quick and slow tests"* on page 111. If basic tests are not passing, the complete build should fail. Ideally, this should stop people from committing unchecked code into the repository. In practice, however, unchecked code does somehow find its way into the source code repository from time to time. I strongly suggest setting the build server to run all quick tests after any code change in the repository, to get the fastest feedback.

Component and integration tests run more slowly so it is not practical to run them on every change. We typically execute them every couple of hours on a central system, so developers don't have to care about them. The build system should, however, fail and notify developers when one of these tests fail (and it is *when*, not *if*).

Tests that guide the development process typically do not pass for most of the time. When they all pass, the work is done. So, there's no reason to sound the fire alarm when an acceptance test fails. However, publishing acceptance test results periodically is a good idea, because it helps to answer the most frequent question we get from project managers: "how are we doing?".

Stuff to remember

- There are several options to set up FitNesse for a team environment. You can use a single central server, remote wiki import with local FitNesse instances or store test files in an external version control system.
- Having a central server makes sense even if you store files in an external version control system, so that business people can use FitNesse without installing anything.
- Use Windows resource kit utilities to set up FitNesse as a system service on the central server.
- Deploy DLLs in the folder where your test runner is to make sure that reflection and serialisation works.
- Integrate FitNesse into your automated build process so that tests are executed even when people forget to do that.
- Don't mix quick and slow tests so that developers can run through basic verifications on every change.
- Separate code-oriented and customer-oriented tests so that non-technical people do not get confused.
- Use the root page to configure FitNesse for running .NET tests by default.
- When integrating with continuous build tools, make sure to delete old test results so that they do not get mixed with new ones.
- FitNesse.NET test runner does not produce XML results in the format that CruiseControl expects, so you have to reformat them using the Java test runner.

Chapter 11.

Testing web interfaces

FitNesse allows clients and non-technical people to contribute to testing. Since they mostly deal with end-user interfaces, the question of writing user interface tests with FitNesse comes up often. FitNesse and FIT do not support the testing of user interfaces out of the box, but they can integrate nicely with other tools for this job. This allows us to use the functionality of UI-specific test frameworks, but keep all the benefits of FitNesse such as being able to write tests in plain English. In this chapter we find out how one such framework can be integrated with FIT and FitNesse to automate web user interface testing.

Choosing the right thing to test

The user interface is typically the most volatile part of a software package. It is heavily influenced by workflow rules and usability constraints, not to mention all the eye candy intended to seduce potential buyers. Maintaining UI-specific tests and keeping up with all the layout changes requires a lot of effort, so the benefits of user interface tests are rarely on the same level as the benefits of business domain tests.

However, a few cleverly chosen web UI tests can make our work a lot easier. The trick is to focus on the right things to test. Because of the workflow constraints, it is hard to peel the onion and get to business rules and objects. Testing the business domain through the UI is probably not the best choice. Acceptance tests for business rules are much easier to write and maintain when they work beneath the user interface. Usability and exploratory tests are typically done on the user interfaces, but they are hard to automate. Checking whether something is usable or not requires a human touch, because usability is subjective. Exploratory tests are random in nature and are not a good candidate for automation.

There are, however, two types of GUI tests that it makes sense to automate:

- Workflow and session control tests
- Face-saving tests

User interface tests should mostly be focused on the customer experience and benefits. With FitNesse they can look almost like a user manual. These tests are good candidates for your clients to write on their own, if you can get them involved.

Don't waste too much time on UI tests

It makes no sense to go into unit-level detail with UI tests for most applications. Business logic and all functionality should typically be enclosed (and tested) in the lower layers of the system. Having said that, there are examples of applications where UI logic and the workflow are major selling points (like video games). It's up to you to decide how much of the user interface should be covered by tests. In general, the more tests the better, but don't waste your time. In most cases, it is better to spend time cleaning up the code or writing more business rule tests than to spend time trying to get 100% UI test coverage.

With web UIs, tests run significantly slower then if they were connecting directly to business classes. So these tests should definitely be avoided in the basic test suite that people must run on every code change. This is one more argument for testing business logic beneath the UI, not with it.

Workflow and session control

Workflow control is typically handled in a layer above business rules, so we have to use a test suite focused on the user interface to verify important parts of the workflow. This includes session control: checking whether pages refuse access if a user is not logged in or does not have a certain security role.

Face-saving tests

In practice, the UI layer is not subject to as many tests as other layers, because we focus on testing business rules. But the user interface is the only thing that customers actually see and experience. A silly UI problem, like a misspelled URL in the login form, can effectively prevent people from doing anything useful with the system. Although such mistakes can be corrected relatively quickly, they are quite embarrassing. Mistakes like this do happen. That's why I recommend always running a quick human test on a system before the release, even if the code is completely covered by tests. Automating key usage scenarios to verify the full path from the GUI down to the database also helps, because automated scripts can be checked every day. These tests should not replace the half-hour human test before the release, but they are a useful aid that can provide early warnings of problems. I call these tests face-saving,[1] because their primary goal is to prevent embarrassment.

In our test application, key business scenarios might be logging in from the home page and purchasing a ticket for the next draw.

Web site code

Web development is not the subject of this book, so I am not going to explain how to develop web sites or actually go through building one for this chapter. The goal of this chapter is to show how to test web pages in practice. So we are going to use a very simple web page with a login form, and a dynamic handler that verifies the username and password. If you want to look at the code actually used in this example, see section *"Web code"* on page 215.

Test a key business workflow

So, let's do a test for one of our key business workflows. Here's what we want to automate:

1. User opens URL *http://localhost:7711/* (which is where our test site is)

2. User types *testuser* into *username* field

3. User types *testpassword* into *password* field

4. User clicks *Login*

5. Page reloads in less than three seconds

6. Page contains text *You have logged in*

Introducing Selenium

Web user interfaces have traditionally been hard to integrate into an automated test process. *Selenium* and FitNesse together solve this task incredibly well.

---

[1] See http://gojko.net/2007/09/25/effective-user-interface-testing/ for a more detailed discussion of face-saving tests.

Selenium is an opensource browser automation and testing library, written by the people at ThoughtWorks. It can load pages into the browser, type text into fields, click buttons and links and check page contents.

The core of Selenium is written in JavaScript and HTML and it is compatible with all major browsers, including Internet Explorer and Firefox on Windows,[2] Linux and Mac.

Selenium Remote Control provides the glue between the browser automation engine and .NET, Java or Python code and enables us to write and run Selenium tests in almost all popular test frameworks. FitNesse is a good choice for the second side of this coin because it enables tests to be written almost in English. As the UI is what the clients see, tests can and should be written so that they can verify them.

Setting up Selenium and Remote Control

First, download Selenium Remote Control (it contains the Selenium package as well) from http://www.openqa.org/selenium-rc. Unpack the Remote Control files somewhere on your disk and then start the server by executing **java -jar selenium-server.jar** from the server folder of the package. The server starts on port 4444 by default. If this port is already taken, change it by adding **-port number** to the command line.

It might be convenient to put Selenium Remote Control on a separate server and run it as a windows service, so that developers do not have to start it on their machines. See tip *"Can FitNesse start automatically with Windows?"* on page 112 for instructions on how to do this.

Selenium works by embedding control scripts into an HTML frame and automating actions in another frame with these scripts. This may clash with Internet Explorer and Firefox security rules if the frames do not come from the same domain. Selenium Remote Control works around this limitation by tweaking browser security settings on start-up.

If you do not want to use cross-domain scripting (or want to use a browser that Remote Control cannot tweak), download the Selenium core scripts from http://www.openqa.org/selenium-core and install them into your test web site. Map the core directory from the archive to

---

[2] Selenium works with XP and 2003 straight out of the box, but in Windows 2000 you'll have to tweak the registry to operate Internet Explorer. See http://wiki.openqa.org/display/SRC/Windows+Registry+Support for more information. Selenium works with Firefox on all platforms.

the selenium-server virtual path on the server so that *RemoteRunner.html* is available on */selenium-server/RemoteRunner.html*.

 What is cross-domain scripting?

Cross-domain scripting means allowing a script from one domain to access page details from another domain and is typically considered a security threat[3] However, this is the easiest way to get a browser to perform automatic actions for any web site.

A quick Selenium example

Let's do a quick test to make sure that Selenium Remote Control (RC) is working, before we integrate it with Fitnesse. We'll write a small console application that calls Remote Control, which then opens Google in a browser window, types "Fitnesse" in the search field and clicks the **Search** button.

Create a new .NET project, add a reference to thoughtworks.selenium. core.dll, which you can find in the dotnet folder of Remote Control installation, and then create this class:

For full code, see SeleniumTest/Console.cs on page 175

```
1   using System;
2   using Selenium;
3   namespace SeleniumTest
4   {
5     class Console
6     {
7       static void Main(string[] args)
8       {
9         ISelenium sel = new DefaultSelenium("localhost",
10        4444, "*iehta", "http://www.google.com");
11        sel.Start();
12        sel.Open("http://www.google.com/");
13        sel.Type("q", "FitNesse");
14        sel.Click("btnG");
15        sel.WaitForPageToLoad("3000");
16      }
17    }
18  }
```

Make sure that Selenium RC is running, close all Internet Explorer windows and then execute the program. Selenium RC opens a new IE window (it may be minimised on start, but you should see a new button in the task bar), goes to Google and executes a search.

The Selenium window (Figure 11.1) has three frames. The top-left frame enables you to view the log and debug the execution by examining the DOM tree. The top-right frame displays the last four executed Selenium commands; this comes in useful when troubleshooting tests. The central frame contains the tested page.

Figure 11.1. Selenium Test Window

Using ISelenium

The first statement in the Google example initialises an ISelenium instance. This object is used to control the browser. The first two arguments of the constructor specify the host and port of the Remote Control server. In this case the Remote Control server is on localhost port 4444. The third constructor argument is a browser string. In this case it is *iehta, the code for Internet Explorer tweaked to allow cross-domain scripting. Use *chrome for Firefox with cross-domain scripting, or *iexplore, *firefox and *opera for Internet Explorer, Firefox and Opera without cross-domain security tweaks. You can also specify a full path to the executable instead of these special keywords. The fourth constructor argument is the URL to the test site. It is important only if you do not use cross-domain scripting, but want Selenium to run the scripts from the local domain. In this case, since http://www.google.com is the fourth parameter, Selenium tries to get the files from http://www.google.com/selenium-server/RemoteRunner.html. Since Google does not host a Selenium installation, it runs the local scripts instead. You always need to specify this argument, so just set it to some existing site if you use cross-domain scripting.

As you can guess from the names, method `Type` simulates the entry of data from the keyboard into a text field and `Click` simulates a mouse click. We access the text field and the button by their names, q and btnG. Selenium can also find elements by their ID (prefix with `identifier=`), XPath expression (prefix with `xpath=`), a DOM path or a CSS property. See http://www.openqa.org/selenium-core/reference.html for more information on locators.

Connecting from FitNesse

Instead of writing a new fixture type for every page or web site, let's write a generic `WebTest` fixture and then describe the test scripts in FitNesse pages. We'll extend `DoFixture`, so that other fixtures can be easily embedded into it, for checking the back-end data after a web script, or preparing the stage for the web test. I break the class into smaller parts to explain it in detail. See all the code in section *"webfixture/WebTest.cs"* on page 200 or download it from http://gojko.net/fitnesse.

Starting and stopping the browser

At the start of a test, we have to open a browser and set up the Selenium environment from the test fixture. To keep the test script format in English-like prose, we'll use the following syntax:

For full code, see LoginTest on page 203

```
3   !|Start Browser|*iehta|With Selenium Console On| localhost| At Port |
4444|And Scripts At|http://localhost:7711|
```

We'll keep the active `ISelenium` instance as a local `instance` field in our `WebTest` fixture, so this method starts the browser:

For full code, see webfixture/WebTest.cs on page 200

```
11      public void StartBrowserWithSeleniumConsoleOnAtPortAndScriptsAt(
```

```
12              String browser, String rcServer, int rcPort, String
 seleniumURL)
13          {
14              instance = new DefaultSelenium(rcServer,
15                                  rcPort, browser,
 seleniumURL);
16              instance.Start();
17          }
```

At the end of each test, we need to shut down the browser, so that Selenium RC does not run out of resources. For this, we'll call the Selenium Stop method:

For full code, see webfixture/WebTest.cs on page 200

```
18          public void ShutdownBrowser()
19          {
20              instance.Stop();
21          }
```

These two methods can be called from *SetUp* and *TearDown* pages, so that individual tests can focus on the actual workflow under test.

Hide browser codes

To make web test pages really customer-friendly, you can use browser names or shortcuts in the page, and then map those to browser codes like *iehta in the fixture class.

Simulating client interaction

The first action in our test script is to navigate to the test page. As in the Google example, we can use the Selenium method Open to point the browser in the right direction:

For full code, see webfixture/WebTest.cs on page 200

```
47          public void UserOpensURL(String s)
48          {
49              instance.Open(s);
50          }
```

Next, we need to implement methods that simulate button clicks and text input. To achieve the best effect, the script must relate to what users see on the screen. However, this is easier said than done. Text fields, check boxes and buttons are all instances of input elements. Although text fields are mostly distinguished by their names, button names are typically not important and users only see the value attribute of a button. So, our WebTest fixture must look for various combinations of attributes. For example, when searching for a button it should first look for an input element with type submit or button and a name attribute matching the query. If no such element is found, it should look for a similar element with a value attribute matching the query. Finally, it should look for a button with a matching DOM ID. We can use XPath to describe expressions for all these combinations and then check them in sequence:

For full code, see webfixture/WebTest.cs on page 200

```
22      public static readonly string[] buttonLocators = new String[] {
23      "xpath=//input[@type='submit' and @name='{0}']",
24      "xpath=//input[@type='button' and @name='{0}']",
25      "xpath=//input[@type='submit' and @value='{0}']",
26      "xpath=//input[@type='button' and @value='{0}']",
27      "xpath=//input[@type='submit' and @id='{0}']",
28      "xpath=//input[@type='button' and @id='{0}']"};
```

Although looking for an element by ID or name would be quicker, we intentionally use XPath and add extra information to catch errors caused by wrong element types. This means that tests run more slowly, but have more precision. To check whether an element exists in the page, we can use the IsElementPresent method of ISelenium. Here is code that uses IsElementPresent to run through an array of locators and return the first matching element:

For full code, see webfixture/WebTest.cs on page 200

```
34          private String GetLocator(String caption, String[]
   possibleFormats)
35          {
36              foreach (String s in possibleFormats)
37              {
38                  String locator = String.Format(s, caption);
39                  if (instance.IsElementPresent(locator))
40                  {
41                      return locator;
42                  }
43              }
44              throw new ApplicationException(
45                "Cannot find element by " + caption);
46          }
```

We already know how to use the Click method from the Google example, so let's just wrap it into a nice DoFixture procedure:

For full code, see webfixture/WebTest.cs on page 200

```
64        public void UserClicksOn(String buttonCaption)
65        {
66            instance.Click(GetLocator(buttonCaption, buttonLocators));
67        }
```

The value attribute of a button is visible on the screen, but there is no such property for text fields. Generally we'll have to rely on the name attribute. Since HTML names and IDs cannot contain blanks, let's strip the blanks from the required name. This allows us to map a command like *User types 10109 into security number field* to an element named securitynumber.

For full code, see webfixture/WebTest.cs on page 200

```
51        public static readonly string[] textFieldLocators = new String[]
          {
52        "xpath=//input[@type='text' and @name='{0}']",
53        "xpath=//input[@type='password' and @name='{0}']",
54        "xpath=//textarea[@name='{0}']",
55        "xpath=//input[@type='text' and @id='{0}']",
56        "xpath=//input[@type='password' and @id='{0}']",
57        "xpath=//textarea[@id='{0}']"};
58
59        public void UserTypesIntoField(String what, String where)
60        {
61            instance.Type(GetLocator(
62            where.Replace(" ", ""), textFieldLocators), what);
63        }
```

Inspecting results

With web tests, we typically want to check that the result was correct and that the site responded quickly enough. The Selenium method WaitForPageToLoad can be used to check whether a page loads in any given amount of time. The API is a bit weird, as it expects a string containing the number of milliseconds. Let's wrap it into a DoFixture method:

For full code, see webfixture/WebTest.cs on page 200

```
68        public void PageReloadsInLessThanSeconds(String sec)
69        {
```

```
70                    instance.WaitForPageToLoad(sec + "000");
71        }
```

Finally, we need a method to verify that page contents are correct. The Selenium method IsTextPresent can help with this:

For full code, see webfixture/WebTest.cs on page 200

```
72        public bool PageContainsText(String s)
73        {
74            return instance.IsTextPresent(s);
75        }
```

What about Ajax?

Waiting for the page to reload is not applicable to testing Ajax (Web 2.0) sites. Instead, describe your acceptance criteria with a JavaScript expression and use the WaitForCondition method to wait until the expression becomes true. Remember that the Selenium script is executed in a different frame, so referencing DOM elements and JS functions in your test site page does not work straight away. Prefix the references with selenium.browserbot.getCurrentWindow() to get from the Selenium frame to your test page. Here's an example:

```
instance.WaitForCondition(
    "(selenium.browserbot.getCurrentWindow().get_username()!
=null)",
    timeout);
```

Completing the test

Now we can turn the script from section *"Test a key business workflow"* on page 123 into a FitNesse test:

For full code, see LoginTest on page 203

```
1   !|webfixture.WebTest|
2
3   !|Start Browser|*iehta|With Selenium Console On| localhost| At Port |
4444|And Scripts At|http://localhost:7711|
4
5   |User Opens URL|http://localhost:7711/login.aspx|
6   |User types|testuser|into|username|field|
7   |User types|testpassword|into|password|field|
```

```
8
9   |User clicks on|Log In|
10  |Page reloads in less than|3|seconds|
11  |Page contains text|You have logged in|
12
13  |Shutdown browser|
```

When you execute this test, it connects to Selenium RC, opens a browser window, tries to log in and checks the page content to verify results (Figure 11.2).

Why did IE stop working after the test?

If Selenium Remote Control does not shut down correctly, or you don't close the browser window, IE might keep the connection settings set by Selenium during tests. This can also affect MSN messenger and other programs that use an embedded IE browser. Go to Tools, Internet Options, Connections, LAN Settings and check whether the Selenium file is still being used as the automatic configuration script (see image below). Uncheck the box and IE should start working again.

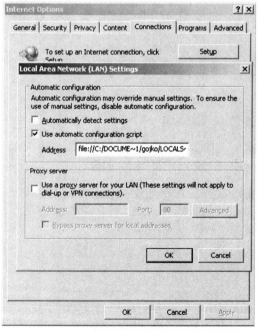

Figure 11.2. A Selenium test works straight from FitNesse

Running tests on a remote server

Selenium RC tries to open a new browser session with different security settings, but under the profile of the current user (in fact, the user that started Remote Control). This may cause problems when you already have an open browser on the same machine. The workaround is to use a different browser for testing. For example, I use Firefox for normal browsing, so Remote Control can start Internet Explorer and play with it. But, there is a much better solution.

As the name suggests, Remote Control can run on a remote dedicated test server and be accessed by developers from their own machines. In that case, Remote Control opens browsers on the remote (dedicated) server, not on developer machines. This enables us to continue using browsers for other tasks on our machines while running UI tests. It also enables us to re-use the same FitNesse scripts to check how various browsers behave on different platforms. We can use symbolic links (see section *"Reuse entire suites with symbolic links"* on page 75) to create test suites for different browsers and environments but maintain scripts in one place.

More Selenium tests

This example was just to get you started with Selenium. This tool can simulate quite a few operations and inspect various page properties. For example, use the Select method to choose options from a dropdown menu (select HTML tag), or GetLocation to inspect the current page URL. See dotnet/doc/index.html in your Remote Control installation for more information on the ISelenium interface.

Stuff to remember

- Web UI tests can be quite brittle and it may take a lot of effort to maintain them and keep up with all the changes, so they are best used to automate a few key scenarios.
- Selenium can be used to simulate user actions and inspect Web page details and content.
- Remote Control can execute Selenium tests on various platforms.

Chapter 12.

Testing database code

Even for projects where the database is used just as a simple persistence layer, it has an impact on automated tests. Integration and acceptance tests should run in an environment as close to the production environment as possible, which today often involves a database. This means that data needs to be set up before the test, cleaned up after, and that changes to data may need to be verified in the database. Writing code to do this in .NET is not rocket science, but it is dull and error-prone, and I'd rather avoid it.

DbFit is an extension library to FIT that enables tests to be executed directly against a database. DbFit fixtures take care of all the database integration plumbing, including automated transaction management, parameter declarations and selecting the right column or parameter type. Because of this, it is easier to write database tests with DbFit than it is to implement manual validations.

To use DbFit fixtures in your tests, download the *dbfit-dotnet-binaries* package from http://sourceforge.net/projects/dbfit. To install it, unpack the ZIP and copy dbfit.dll into the FIT.NET folder. If you installed FitNesse as suggested in section *"Setting up FitNesse"* on page 13, this is the dotnet2 folder in your main FitNesse directory.

Connecting to the database

DbFit fixtures can work in two modes:

- In flow mode: a DatabaseTest fixture controls the whole page and coordinates testing. You can use other fixtures as well, but no other fixture can take over flow mode processing. In flow mode, DbFit automatically rolls back the current transaction at the end to make tests repeatable, and provides some additional options such as inspections of stored procedure error results.
- Standalone: you can use individual fixtures without having DatabaseTest coordinate the whole page. In this case, you are responsible for transaction management. This enables you to have more control over the database testing process, and even supply your own database connection to make sure that .NET integration tests are running in the same transaction.

The mode in which you are using DbFit fixtures affects how you connect to the database.

Which mode should I use?

If you can, use flow mode. It gives you automatic transaction management and some other shortcuts. If your test relies on some other fixture controlling the page in flow mode, use standalone fixtures. The syntax is, in most cases, absolutely the same.

Connecting in flow mode

In flow mode, the current database connection is kept in a protected field of the DatabaseTest instance. SqlServerTest is a subclass of DatabaseTest that just initialises it to work with SqlServer 2005.

Use the Connect method to initialise the database connection. Pass the server (optionally followed by the instance name), username, password and the database name as arguments. This is how I connect to a SqlServer 2005 Express[1] instance on my laptop:

```
!|dbfit.SqlServerTest|

!|Connect|LAPTOP\SQLEXPRESS|FitNesseUser|Password|TestDB|
```

If you are connecting to a default database, you can omit the fourth parameter. If you want to use non-standard connection properties, or initialise your connection differently (for example, using Windows integrated authentication), call Connect with a single argument — the full .NET connection string. Here is an example:

```
|Connect|data source=Instance;user id=User;password=Pwd;database=TestDB;|
```

For flow mode to work correctly, the SqlServerTest fixture must be the first one on the page — not even import can be before it. This is why we explicitly specify the namespace.

---

[1] free version of SqlServer 2005 for developers. See http://www.microsoft.com/sql/editions/express/.

Connecting in standalone mode

In standalone mode, the connection properties are stored in the public
DefaultEnvironment **singleton field inside** dbfit.DbEnvironmentFactory. **You**
can initialise it from your own fixtures if you want to pass an existing database connection (to make sure that your .NET tests are using
the same transaction as DbFit fixtures). Alternatively, you can use the
DatabaseEnvironment **fixture from the** dbfit.fixture **package to define the**
connection. To change the default environment (or initialise it for the
first time), pass the new environment type as the first argument to
the fixture. For SqlServer 2005, the value of this argument should be
SQLSERVER. DatabaseEnvironment **is a** SequenceFixture (see tip *"Can I use
flow mode without weird method names?"* on page 88) that wraps the
DefaultEnvironment **singleton as a system under test, so that you can**
then call all its public methods directly — including the Connect method
explained earlier.

```
|import|
|dbfit.fixture|

!|DatabaseEnvironment|sqlserver|
|Connect|LAPTOP\SQLEXPRESS|FitNesseUser|Password|TestDB|
```

Notice that there is no space between DatabaseEnvironment **and** Connect
— they have to be in the same table. Because we are not using flow
mode, we can use the import fixture as well. Most DbFit fixtures are in
dbfit.fixture **namespace, so it is good practice to include this names-**
pace.

Can I use both modes in the same test suite?

Yes, in different tests. Note that the imported namespace
may give you some problems in flow mode. If you want to
mix and match, then either do not import the dbfit.fixture
namespace for standalone tests, or use the utility Export
fixture to cancel the namespace import after the standalone
test.

```
!|dbfit.util.Export|
|dbfit.fixture|
```

Transaction management

In flow mode, the current transaction is automatically rolled back at the end of the page. If you want to commit it to make changes permanent, put the Commit table into the page. There are no arguments or additional parameters — the table contents contain just this one word. Likewise, you can roll back manually in your test using the Rollback table.

In standalone mode, use the DatabaseEnvironment fixture again, but do not specify a fixture argument. This tells the DatabaseEnvironment to use the current default database connection, without attempting to initialise it. Call Commit or Rollback in the second row.

```
!|DatabaseEnvironment|
|rollback|
```

It is a very good idea to put this table in a *TearDown* page for your test suite when you use standalone DbFit fixtures. This will make sure that your tests are repeatable.

Fixtures and methods

All the fixtures described in the rest of this chapter are in the dbfit.fixture namespace. In flow mode, do not use the fixtures directly, but instead call methods of the DatabaseTest class. The appropriate methods have the same names as the fixtures they relate to. If you import the namespace for standalone fixtures, the table syntax in both modes is absolutely the same.

Working with stored procedures

To test or execute a stored procedure, use the ExecuteProcedure fixture. ExecuteProcedure works like a ColumnFixture, and expects the procedure name as the first argument. Input and output parameters are listed in the second table row. As usual with ColumnFixture, each output parameter must be followed by a question mark. All rows after the second one specify test values for input parameters and expected values for output parameters. When we run the test, DbFit calls the procedure for every combination of input parameters, and verifies that output parameter values match what we expect. Here is a simple example. If the word concatenation in the Hello World example (section *"A quick test"* on page 15) was implemented as a stored procedure, this would be the test for it:

```
!|Execute Procedure|ConcatenateStrings|
|firststring|secondstring|concatenated?|
|Hello|World|Hello World|
```

Now you can see how easy it is to write a stored procedure test. The boilerplate code is absolutely minimal. There are no variable declarations and no exception handlers. You don't have to know the data type of parameters. You can use this fixture to test database stored procedures, but also to call a stored procedure quickly during a .NET data-driven test. To test or call stored functions, create a column with only a question mark in the header. Use this column for the function result, just as you use other columns for parameters.

Note that all other FitNesse features, such as symbols and markup variables, work with DbFit fixtures as well.

Can I use DbFit with a different database?

In this book, I use Sql Server 2005 examples because this is what most people use with .NET. DbFit also supports Oracle 9 and later versions and MySql 5 (only in the Java version) out of the box. If your database is not one of these, you can still use DbFit with a bit of effort.

DbFit fixtures use an abstraction for the database engine represented by the dbfit.IDBEnvironment interface. This interface is relatively simple and it should not take you more than four to five hours to implement it for your particular database. DbFit is open-source so you can even take a peek at SqlServerEnvironment and OracleEnvironment implementations to help you get started with the task. See http://dbfit.svn.sourceforge.net/svnroot/dbfit/dbfit/impl/dotnet/src/environment/ for more details.

If you cannot do this yourself, contact me and I'll help.

Preparing test data

Insert is the database equivalent of SetUpFixture (see section *"Use SetUp-Fixture to prepare the stage for tests"* on page 83), and can be used to populate tables with data quickly. Specify the table name as the first fixture argument, then define the data structure in the second row and specify data in subsequent rows:

```
!|Insert|Users|
|username|name|
|pete|Peter Pan|
|mike|Michael Jordan|
```

The `Insert` fixture can also return automatically generated columns, such as primary key values. Use a question mark after the column name to specify that a column should be read from the database. You can store the output into fixture symbols for later use:

```
!|Insert|Users|
|username|name|userid?|
|pete|Peter Pan|>>user1|
|mike|Michael Jordan|>>user2|
```

Executing statements

To execute an SQL statement quickly, use the `Execute` fixture and specify the statement in the second cell. This fixture does not have any additional rows. Bound variables in statements are automatically linked to fixture symbols. For example, the following table updates the user whose ID is stored into the `user2` symbol. Note that a different syntax is used to access symbols — SQLServer uses @ to mark bound variables, and you should use this instead of << and >>.

```
!|Execute| Update Users set name='Michael Jackson' where userid=@user2|
```

To execute multi-line statements, enclose them inside `!-` and `-!` so that FitNesse knows to treat the whole statement as one cell.

Verifying query results

The `Query` fixture is the database equivalent of `RowFixture`. Specify the query statement as the first fixture argument, then put the output structure in the second row and list expected results in subsequent rows. You can use partial row-key mapping (see section *"Use RowFixture for better precision"* on page 101) by putting a question mark next to columns that do not belong to the primary key. Just as with SQL statements, bound variables are automatically read from fixture symbols. You can also use symbols for data comparisons.

```
|Query|Select * from users where userid<@lastid|
|userid|username?|name?|
|<<user1|pete|Peter Pan|
|<<user2|mike|Michael Jordan|
```

Database unit testing

Although FitNesse is generally intended for story tests and acceptance testing and not unit-level functional verifications, with the assistance of DbFit it becomes an easy-to-use tool for database unit tests. Because the tabular test format is very close to the relational data model, FIT tests do not suffer from the object model-relational data model mismatch that renders most xUnit-style tools effectively unusable for database testing. In fact, one of the goals of DbFit is to enable the use of FitNesse for effective database acceptance and unit testing by database developers with no .NET or Java knowledge.

To help database developers get started with unit testing, DbFit releases contain a *dbfit-complete* package as well. This package brings together the latest release of FitNesse, the latest version of FIT.NET, and the DbFit binaries, ready to use. The default wiki site in this package contains a lot of examples of how to use DbFit fixtures. If you are interested in DbFit, I suggest that you download this package first and browse through the wiki pages — especially the *DotNet.AcceptanceTests* test suite.

There is also a PDF guide intended to help database developers make the most of DbFit without learning any .NET or Java skills. You can download it from http://gojko.net/fitnesse/dbfit.

Other DbFit features

DbFit has more useful fixtures. The Inspect fixture can be used to quickly build a regression test for a query, or to read out metadata from the database and create a test template based on a stored procedure, table or view. The Update fixture allows you to modify existing records in a tabular form, without writing the statement manually. Clean helps with deleting data and QueryStats allows you to inspect statistics about a query without actually specifying the result data. StoreQuery and CompareStored-Queries allow you to compare the results of two queries dynamically.

This is as far as we will go in explaining DbFit, because this book is not about database testing. However, if this topic interests you, see the Dbfit project web site http://www.dbfit.org for more examples and a reference guide to other DbFIt fixtures. Scott W. Ambler also has a lot of good advice on applying agile practices to databases on http://www.agiledata.org.

Stuff to remember

- DbFit fixtures can work in flow mode or in standalone mode. Flow mode automatically controls transactions and has some other helpful shortcuts. Standalone mode gives you more control.
- Use the Insert fixture to prepare the stage quickly for data-driven .NET integration tests.
- Use the Query fixture to verify the database state after a data-driven .NET integration test or the execution of a stored procedure.
- Use the ExecuteProcedure fixture to test stored procedures or quickly script a stored procedure call for a .NET integration test.
- Use the Execute fixture to execute any database statement.
- FitNesse symbols are automatically mapped to database bound variables.

Chapter 13.

Testing legacy code

Maintaining a legacy system is often compared to walking through a swamp. Any move we make is incredibly slow and we don't really know what we are stepping into. Being afraid of the next step and unwilling to make any changes is the essence of working with legacy for me. Although the primary goal of FIT and FitNesse is to help with acceptance tests, these tools have some great features for testing legacy code.

Covering legacy code with tests

Michael Feathers[1] suggests that the first step when dealing with legacy code is to cover it with tests, so that we will not be afraid to change it. Feathers goes so far as to call any code without test support legacy: "The main thing that distinguishes legacy code from non-legacy code is tests, or rather a lack of tests." Although the word legacy has a different meaning for me, I still have a very uneasy gut feeling when new software is being developed without proper test support.

When TDD practices are used, tests represent what Feathers calls an "invariant on the code", something we can rely on to tell us when the functionality has changed. We should first build this invariant and then get on with improving the code. So, the first step is actually getting some useful test cases for the code. Don't bother too much with calculating correct test outputs. As Feathers puts it, "The key thing is that correct behaviour is defined by what the set of classes did yesterday, not by any external standard of correctness". We need to create tests that verify current functionality and then use them to check future changes.

FitNesse can help a lot in this task, by allowing us to take a quick snapshot of the current functionality and convert it into tests.

Use blank cells to print out results

Fixture classes from the basic FIT package (including `ColumnFixture`, `ActionFixture` and `RowFixture`) handle a blank check cell by printing out

---

[1] See his book Working Effectively With Legacy Code [5]. A short online introduction into this subject is on http://www.objectmentor.com/resources/articles/WorkingEffectivelyWithLegacyCode.pdf

the actual result, without comparing it to anything. We can write a test without actually specifying the results and FitNesse will print current values when we run this test. We can now quickly turn these results into a new test and use the values as expected outcome for the future.

To convert the results into a test, select the entire table in the browser, directly from the rendered results page, not from the HTML source nor wiki source, and copy it. Internet Explorer allows you to get just a few rows at a time, while in some versions of Firefox you have to select the entire table in order to copy it properly. Edit the test page, delete the old table and paste the contents of the clipboard into the page editor. You should see the results table with column values separated by tabs. Click the **Spreadsheet to FitNesse** button below the editor text box. This turns the tab-separated results table into a FitNesse test table, converting the tabs into pipes to separate cells and even putting the exclamation mark before the first row automatically. Simply save the page and you have a snapshot test.

Use Word and Excel to write tests

The **Spreadsheet to FitNesse** button is used in the examples in this chapter to convert tables on the clipboard into FitNesse tests. It was originally included to allow non-technical people such as clients and business analysts to write tests without learning wiki markup syntax; they tend to appreciate the option to write tests in Excel or Word. You can just copy tables from Excel and paste them into the FitNesse page editor (or, even better, get business analysts to do this) and click that magic button to get an instant test. To edit a test in Excel, first click **FitNesse to Spreadsheet** to convert pipes into tabs, then copy the content back into Excel and fire away.

Use show and check with FitLibrary

FitLibrary fixtures (DoFixture and SequenceFixture) do not handle blank cells like basic FIT fixtures. Trying to compare with a blank string will probably cause an "Input string was not in correct format" error. However, creating a snapshot of the current functionality with FitLibrary classes is not much harder than with FIT fixtures. First use the show keyword in the test, run it to display the actual results of test methods, then copy the results into any text editor (Notepad will do just fine). Replace show with check. Then just convert the result into a a test table with **Spreadsheet to FitNesse**.

Although you don't need to use the check keyword to test boolean methods with DoFixture and SequenceFixture (see section *"Use DoFixture keywords for better control"* on page 66), you do need the show/ check combination to snapshot the functionality correctly. Using these keywords makes FitNesse explicitly display the result instead of just checking whether it is true.

Wrap existing objects for tests

FitNesse allows us to use existing business objects straightaway with fixtures. Using ready-made objects can save a lot of time and effort when testing an existing code base. We can use GetTargetObject to wrap a business interface with basic FIT fixtures (see section *"Use data-transfer objects directly"* on page 52), or use mySystemUnderTest to do the same with FIT library fixtures (see section *"Wrapping business objects with DoFixture"* on page 90). You can then use the methods and properties of business objects directly in your test tables. SequenceFixture is perhaps the best choice for wrapping service classes, and ColumnFixture would probably be the best for data-oriented classes. Of course, mix this with automatic array and list conversion into ArrayFixture to get the best results (see section *"Testing lists of objects"* on page 94).

Don't reimplement business interfaces

When covering legacy code with FitNesse tests, watch out for fixtures that reimplement your business interfaces (especially data-transfer interfaces) and always refactor them to wrap around appropriate default implementations (see section *"Use data-transfer objects directly"* on page 52). You might be able to drop most fixture methods completely and use automatic method wrapping with DoFixture and SequenceFixture (see section *"Wrapping business objects with DoFixture"* on page 90 and tip *"Can I use flow mode without weird method names?"* on page 88). Also see section *"Avoid conversions by supporting custom data types"* on page 159 for further ideas on how to reduce the amount of your fixture code.

Treat fixtures like the rest of your code and fight against unnecessary duplication. Having ten additional fields and methods in a fixture only makes it harder to maintain. If the fixture just acts as a wrapper over the business class, the code is much easier to maintain.

Use ArrayFixture and RowFixture to capture data batches

To snapshot data batches with `ArrayFixture` and `RowFixture`, write tests without putting in any expected results. You still have to set up the object structure in the second row (see section *"Use RowFixture for better precision"* on page 101). Run the test to make it fail; FitNesse prints the current results of test methods as surplus rows. Just copy the results into a text editor and remove the `surplus` keyword (by globally replacing it with an empty string). Then copy the new table into the page, again using **Spreadsheet to FitNesse** to convert it into a test automatically.

Remember that the order of elements is important with `ArrayFixture`. If the order can change, for example if data is read from a database without the order by clause, it is better to use `RowFixture` or `SetFixture` instead (see sidebar *"Beware of unstable tests"* on page 146).

Beware of unstable tests

Tests that pass under some circumstances and fail under others cause more harm than good. You really don't want to spend time reading the code and test pages to check whether a test failed because there really was a bug, or because it was raining outside. Avoid writing such tests. When you spot such behaviour, change the tests straight away to be deterministic and reliable or delete them.

Fight against entropy in tests regardless of where it comes from. If the order of elements can change, do not use `ArrayFixture` but `RowFixture` or `SetFixture`, because they ignore element order. A different example of entropy is the false alarm you can get from a continuous integration server when FitNesse freezes. This is why we added a service restart before tests in section *"Integrating FitNesse with CruiseControl.NET"* on page 116, to make test runs more reliable.

Take particular care with tests that depend on the order of execution in a test suite. Although tables on a single page are executed in sequence, there is no guaranteed order for a number of pages in a suite. Move inter-page dependencies into a common setup. This enables you to run tests individually and protect against changes in future FitNesse implementations.

Using existing forms for regression tables

If you already have correct outputs of the business process in forms that can be easily converted to HTML tables, you can use them as FitNesse tests almost straight away. Common examples are MS Word invoices and Excel calculations. You can copy HTML code directly into FitNesse pages (enclose it within !- and -! to prevent wiki formatting). Alternatively, you can use the **Spreadsheet to FitNesse** button to create test tables from old forms in tab-separated format.

Here is a simple example: we want to use an old invoice (Figure 13.1) as a regression test for calculating tax. To connect the invoice to our business code, we can use TableFixture, a fixture class for testing free-form tables. Note that it is in the fitnesse.fixtures namespace, not in fit or fitlibrary like all the classes we have seen so far. To use a TableFixture, we need to implement the DoStaticTable(int rows) method and process our table there. We can get a string or integer in any cell using GetString(int row, int column) and GetInt(int row, int column). Tests that pass should be marked by calling the Right(int row, int column) method and tests that fail should be marked by calling Wrong(int row, int column, string actualValue).

Figure 13.1. We can turn this invoice into a FitNesse test

Item	Product code	Price
Pragmatic Program-mer	B978-0201616224	34.03
Sony RDR-GX330	ERDR-GX330	94.80
Test Driven Develop-ment By Example	B978-0321146533	32.39
Net Total		161.22
Tax (10% on applicable items)		9.48
Total		170.70

We are interested only in the final tax calculation, so we just disregard the rest of the table. Let's check whether the value in the second row from the bottom matches what our tax calculator works out based on the rows in the middle.

For full code, see extended/Invoice.cs on page 199

```
15    public class Invoice:fitnesse.fixtures.TableFixture
16    {
17      protected override void DoStaticTable(int rows)
18      {
19        TaxCalculator tc=new TaxCalculator();
20        decimal totaltax = 0;
21        for (int row = 1; row < rows - 3; row++)
22        {
23          totaltax += tc.GetTax(GetString(row, 1),
24            Decimal.Parse(GetString(row, 2)));
25        }
26        decimal taxintable = Decimal.Parse(GetString(rows - 2, 2));
27        if (taxintable == totaltax)
28          Right(rows - 2, 2);
29        else
30          Wrong(rows - 2, 2, totaltax.ToString());
31      }
32    }
```

The cell that holds the calculated tax (third cell in the second row from
below) is used as a test, while the others are ignored. We can use the
invoice table to run the test (see Figure 13.2).

Figure 13.2. We can test free-form tables with `TableFixture`

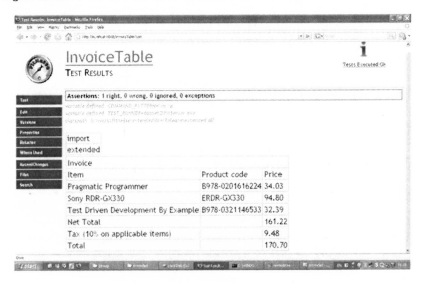

Stuff to remember

- The first step when dealing with legacy code is to cover it with tests.
- FitNesse enables you to build regression tests for current functionality quickly.
- Basic FIT fixtures show the current result when the cell is blank.
- Results can be quickly converted to tests with **Spreadsheet to FitNesse**.
- Show and check keywords must be used with DoFixture to snapshot functionality.
- FitNesse can also take plain HTML tables as tests.
- TableFixture is used to test free-form tables.

Chapter 14.

Under the hood

Understanding what really happens during a test allows you to customise FIT and FitNesse to your particular project needs and troubleshoot tests. Now that we've learnt how to use FitNesse, we take a peek under the hood and examine how the FIT engine really works.

What really happens during a test?

FitNesse is just a user interface to FIT. It prepares test pages by converting wiki syntax to HTML, but it does not execute tests internally. Instead, it calls an external FIT runner to execute the tests. FitNesse starts a Java FIT runner by default, but we can change this by modifying the TEST_RUNNER variable. (We did this in section *"How FitNesse connects to .NET classes"* on page 20: we changed the runner to dotnet2\FitServer.exe.) In a .NET environment, FitNesse starts an external FitServer.exe process and passes the test name and FitNesse port as parameters. The FitServer process then connects to FitNesse, downloads the page and executes tests. The results are passed back to FitNesse, which displays them to the user. This is why, when tests are hanging and locking resources, you should look for FitServer.exe processes to kill rather than stopping the Java process that runs FitNesse.

There are a few other test runners that you can use. In Chapter 10, *Working in a team*, we used TestRunner.exe to execute tests from a NAnt script. You can also use FolderRunner.exe to execute tests from HTML files stored on disk.

The parse tree

The test runner first breaks the page into HTML tables, then analyses the tables and creates a *parse tree*. A parse tree is a dynamic representation of the test tables. As the tests are executed, fixtures modify the tree by adding comments ("expected something, actual something else") or creating completely new cells (surplus elements in a RowFixture query). At the end of the tests, FitNesse uses the tree contents to display the results.

Important

You can see the full source code for all FIT.NET classes described in this chapter on https://svn.sourceforge.net/svnroot/fitnessedotnet/trunk/src

Parse tree elements are instances of the Parse class. These elements build a tree by creating linked lists with two properties: More and Parts. More points to the next element on the same level of the hierarchy and Parts points to the first child element. The Tag property contains the HTML tag name, for example table, tr and td. The Body property contains the cell content for td tags, and is typically empty for all other tags. The parse tree for the table from Figure 2.3 is shown in Figure 14.1.

Figure 14.1. Typical table parse tree

TAG	TABLE
BODY	
PARTS	●
MORE	

TAG	TR		TAG	TD
BODY			BODY	HelloWorld.OurFirstTest
PARTS	●		PARTS	
MORE	●		MORE	

TAG	TR		TAG	TD		TAG	TD		TAG	TD
BODY			BODY	String1		BODY	String2		BODY	Concatenate?
PARTS	●		PARTS			PARTS			PARTS	
MORE	●		MORE	●		MORE	●		MORE	

TAG	TR		TAG	TD		TAG	TD		TAG	TD
BODY			BODY	Hello		BODY	World		BODY	Hello World
PARTS	●		PARTS			PARTS			PARTS	
MORE			MORE	●		MORE	●		MORE	

Executing tables

The Fixture class is the main workflow controller and coordinator for tests. It also defines the standard interface for test classes and provides default method implementations. In order to enable subclasses to adjust the test execution, this class contains a lot of virtual methods. Fixtures can implement their own table format and test workflow by overriding these methods.

After the test runner has created the parse tree, an instance of the Fixture class is created and the tree is passed to its DoTables method. The main Fixture then takes the class name from the first cell in the first table and creates an instance of this class. The ProcessTables method of this instance is then called, and the whole parse tree is passed to it. Instantiating another Fixture and then passing the whole tree may seem a bit weird, but this is how DoFixture and similar flow-mode FitLibrary fixtures take over page processing.

In the default implementation, which most fixtures do not override, ProcessTables just iterates over tables (first level of the tree). Each table is processed by loading the class name from the first cell, instantiating the class, loading arguments from the remaining cells in the first row and calling the DoTable method of the new fixture. The appropriate table subtree is passed to this DoTable method.

Note that arguments are not passed to the constructor, so they have to be loaded after the instantiation. If you create your own Fixture subclass, remember that fixture arguments are not accessible to the class constructor so you have to check for them later. DoTable is a good candidate for this.

FitLibrary fixtures turn on flow mode (see section *"Embed fixtures for best results"* on page 82) by overriding ProcessTables and then processing the rest of the page as a single big table.

The default implementation of the DoTable method calls the DoRows method, passing the pointer to the second table row (so DoRows does not receive the first row with fixture type and arguments). The default DoRows implementation iterates through child elements of the parse subtree, which represent table rows, and calls DoRow for each one of them. The default DoRow calls the DoCells method, and this iterates through cells and calls DoCell for each one of them. DoCells also checks whether there was an exception during cell processing or not. Exceptions are recorded in the parse tree by calling the Exception method. By default, DoCell just marks the cell as ignored, by calling the Ignore method.

As you can see, there are quite a few opportunities for subfixtures to take over and implement their particular test workflow. This is why FIT and FitNesse are so flexible.

In addition to Exception and Ignore, there are two more methods that can be called to mark part of a parse tree: Right should be called if a test succeeds, and Wrong should be called if a test fails, optionally passing the actual results, so that they can be displayed.

Binding columns to class members

Let's examine one use case in a bit more detail. ColumnFixture is a general purpose testing class, which we introduced in Chapter 2, *Installing FitNesse*, and explained in more detail in Chapter 4, *Writing basic tests*. It uses the second table row to map columns to properties, methods and fields. The other rows are used as test inputs and expected results. Several other classes, including RowFixture, also use the header row to map test object properties to columns. This common functionality that binds columns to object properties is encapsulated into a common superclass, BoundFixture .

BoundFixture provides a way to bind columns to class members and over-rides DoCell to execute the appropriate cell operation. It does not specify how the columns are bound to fields, but expects subclasses to fill in the required mapping. BoundFixture also overrides DoRow in order to provide one more extension point: Reset. This method is called before each row is processed, allowing subclasses to clear temporary data before the next test execution.

ColumnFixture takes over after the first table row is processed, so it over-rides the DoRows method. It uses the current row (second row in the table) to bind columns to properties of the target class and then calls the Bound-Fixture DoRows method. However, it passes the next row (third one in the table) as the argument. From this point on, the method DoCell method of BoundFixture is called for each cell, and it either puts in data to set up tests or compares expected and actual values to verify results.

Cell operation handlers

BoundFixture and all its subclasses use CellOperation class to access target class properties. This is where symbols (see section *"Use symbols to pass dynamic information"* on page 49) and keywords like exception or blank (see section *"Checking for errors"* on page 55 and sidebar *"Fixture keywords"* on page 56) come into play.

CellOperation class has a static list of cell handlers, which implement the ICellHandler interface. In order to execute a cell operation, the class runs through the list and asks handlers whether they match cell content and data type. The first matching handler is used to execute the cell. For example, SymbolRecallHandler matches cells starting with << and ExceptionKeywordHandler matches cells with the exception keyword.

In Part II we used fields, properties and methods of test objects in the same way. BoundFixture provides the same level of abstraction using the Accessor interface. Various Accessor implementations get or set field values or call methods, hiding the underlying object from us. We can just use Get or Set methods with an accessor to access the underlying value.

You can load and unload handlers dynamically to change the way cells are processed (see section *"Load non-standard cell handlers for simpler comparisons"* on page 157).

Because FitLibrary classes do not use CellOperation handlers by default, these features are not available in DoFixture and similar classes unless you specifically ask for them.

How can I use cell handlers with DoFixture?

Since version 1.3, you can ask for a specific cell handler to be available to FitLibrary fixtures. Use the CellHandlerLoader fixture, but put FitLibrary into the third cell. Here is an example that turns on symbols for DoFixture:

```
!|Cell Handler Loader|
|load|SymbolSaveHandler|FitLibrary|
|load|SymbolRecallHandler|FitLibrary|
```

Handling data types

Most fixtures use the TypeAdapter class to convert cell contents into objects. This class looks for a public static Parse method in the target class and uses it to perform the conversion. It also handles arrays of objects by splitting the comma-separated contents into individual objects and then calling the Parse method to process them.

Attaching the Visual Studio debugger

Although spending less time in the debugger is one of the greatest benefits of automated tests, sometimes you'll have to troubleshoot problems with your fixtures, especially while you're learning how to use FitNesse. Attaching the Visual Studio debugger to the FitNesse process might seem like an obvious solution, but it does not do the trick. FitNesse executes tests by starting an external program (FitServer.exe), which vanishes after the test, so you will not be able to find it in the list of active processes or connect to it. Instead, you can use **TestRunner.exe**, which we used for NAnt integration in section *"Running tests with NAnt"* on page 115.

Open project properties in Visual Studio, go to the debug tab, and choose "start external program" as the start action. Select your main FitNesse folder as the working directory and specify the server name, port and test name as command line arguments. An example of the debug configuration is shown on Figure 14.2. Then start the tests in the debugger normally, by pressing **F5**. You can use breakpoints, watches and other Visual Studio debugger features to inspect your test fixtures at run time. Using the main FitNesse folder as the working directory for debugging makes sure that all the relative paths in the tests keep working correctly. Visual Studio can pick up fixture DLLs even if you move them to a deployment folder, as suggested in section *"Organising the files"* on page 110, but make sure that you also copy the debug information files (pdb).

When in doubt, just print to the console

When you just want to see what's going on quickly, instead of loading the project in the debugger, write to the console as you would do in any .NET console application. FitNesse captures the output and displays an "Output Captured" icon in the top left corner of the test results. Click the icon to view everything that your test classes wrote during tests.

Figure 14.2. Use TestRunner.Exe to debug tests

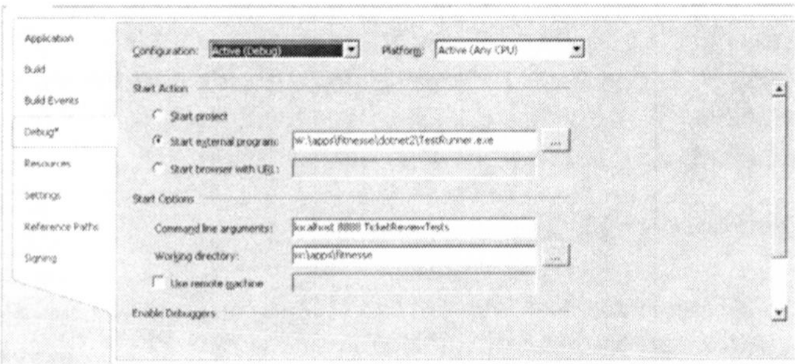

Load non-standard cell handlers for simpler comparisons

Basic FIT fixtures use cell handlers to understand what you write in table cells. For example, the default cell handler just interprets the data literally, but the symbol recall handler looks up the symbol value and uses this instead of the cell contents.

Non-standard cell handlers allow you to write comparisons more easily. For example, sometimes you don't care about the whole string, but just want to check the last few characters. EndsWithHandler allows you to specify the expected results by prefixing the ending with two dots.

EndsWithHandler is not in the list of default handlers, so it must be loaded manually. To load a non-standard handler, create a CellHandlerLoader table. Add rows with the keyword load in the first cell and the class name in second cell. Here is an example:

```
|cell handler loader|
|load|ends with handler|

|String Fixture|
|field|field?|
|Ford Prefect|..ect|
|Marvin|..vin|
```

Non-standard handlers have to be loaded on demand because they can alter the expected behaviour of other functions. When EndsWithHandler is active, two dots at the beginning of a string have a special meaning and they are no longer interpreted literally. To avoid problems, you might want to unload non-standard handlers when the test is over. To do this, use the remove keyword in the CellHandlerLoader table followed by the class name. Two other keywords can be used to manipulate active handlers: the clear keyword drops all active cell handlers and the load-defaults keyword reloads the default handlers.

Here are some other interesting non-standard cell handlers you can use:

IntegralRangeHandler	Checks if a number is in a numeric interval given as min..max
StartsWithHandler	similar to EndsWithHandler, but checks for strings from the left; the syntax is substring..

| SubstringHandler | Checks for substrings anywere; allowed syntax is ..substring, substring.. or ..substring.. |

Simplify verifications with a custom cell handler

Fixtures from the basic FIT package use cell handlers (see section *"Cell operation handlers"* on page 154) to understand the contents of table cells. By implementing a custom handler, you can teach FitNesse how to understand new forms of expressions. For example, the standard FitNesse package for .NET 2 does not allow you to describe a test using a regular expression. If you are testing complex string operations, a custom handler could enable you to write tests much more efficiently.

For customised comparisons, instead of directly implementing the fit.ICellHandler interface, it is better to extend the fitnesse.AbstractCellHandler class. AbstractCellHandler provides default implementations for all interface methods, allowing us to override just what we really need. In this case, we'll implement methods Match (*should our handler be used?*) and HandleEvaluate (*does the actual result match expected?*). Cell handlers are selected based on cell data type and content. In order not to clash with other active handlers, it is best to choose a unique format for the expressions handled by our new class. We'll use enclosure into slashes (/RegEx/), the standard AWK format for regular expressions.

For full code, see extended/RegExHandler.cs on page 199

```
1   using System.Text.RegularExpressions;
2   using fitnesse.handlers;
3   using fit;
4
5   namespace extended
6   {
7     public class RegExHandler: AbstractCellHandler {
8       public override bool Match(string searchString, System.Type type) {
9         return searchString.StartsWith("/") &&
10          searchString.EndsWith("/") &&
11          typeof(string).Equals(type);
12      }
13      public override bool HandleEvaluate(Fixture fixture, Parse cell,
14          Accessor accessor) {
15        object actualValue=accessor.Get(fixture);
16        if (actualValue == null) return false;
```

```
17        Regex expected =new Regex(cell.Text.Substring(1,
cell.Text.Length-2));
18          return expected.IsMatch(actualValue.ToString());
19    }
20  }
21 }
```

We can now check whether strings match regular expressions directly from the tables (Figure 14.3). Remember that you have to load non-standard handlers explicitly.

Figure 14.3. A custom cell handler can simplify comparisons

Cell Handler Loader
load extended.RegExHandler

StringFixture	
field	field?
1938-111-222	/[0-9-]+/
	/[A-Z]+/ *expected*
1938-111-222	
	1938-111-222 *actual*

FitNesse also uses cell handlers to understand keywords like null and blank. If it makes sense to introduce new domain-specific keywords for your project, you can write cell handlers so that FitNesse can understand them.

This technique can also be used to make tables more customer-friendly. In section *"Customer-friendly table"* on page 45 we implemented a test that looked almost exactly like a part of the customer requirements specification. The only thing missing was the currency symbol. The customer's table had a currency symbol next to numbers of dollars and our table did not. We can show FitNesse how to understand the currency symbol with a custom cell handler.

Avoid conversions by supporting custom data types

DoFixture and SequenceFixture allow you to call business domain methods directly from tables (see section *"Wrapping business objects with DoFixture"* on page 90 and tip *"Can I use flow mode without weird method names?"* on page 88) without re-implementing these methods in the fixture. This significantly shortens the effort required to write and maintain tests. However, methods from business classes often handle other business objects, not just basic .NET types. In the second part of the book, we often use a username as a parameter of fixture methods and look for matching Player objects in the fixture code. If our fixture methods mostly convert table contents into business types, we can often simplify the code significantly by telling FitNesse how to create business objects directly. Instead of looking for the Player object every time, a fixture can receive it from the framework. We just need to provide a public static method Parse(String value) that converts strings into our business objects and override ToString and Equals methods to provide consistent conversion to and from strings. FitNesse can then create our business objects on the fly and pass them to methods directly.

Obviously, this cannot be done if the business method arguments are specified by interface, not by class.

What if Parse is not available?

If you want to tell FitNesse how to use a third-party or system object, where you cannot add a Parse method, then you can implement a custom cell handler to provide the conversion.

Implement domain-specific tests using custom fixtures

Most of the time you can extend one of the standard fixtures to define the test workflow, such as ColumnFixture or DoFixture. However, if you find that no existing fixture covers exactly what you need, you might want to implement a completely new table type and use this to describe your domain tests.

For tables without a repetitive structure, extending TableFixture is probably the best solution (see section *"Using existing forms for regression tables"* on page 147). For tables with a clearly repetitive form, it can be more efficient to extend Fixture and just hook in somewhere during the processing, depending on what you want to take over. For processing before the first data row gets executed (for example, connecting to a database specified in Fixture arguments), override DoRows and set up the environment before passing control to the DoRows method of the base class. If you want to process the entire row as a batch, instead of processing individual cells, then override DoRow.

Generally, try to reuse as much as you can. If columns map to object methods and fields in some way, extend BoundFixture (see section *"Binding columns to class members"* on page 154) and implement the correct binding. Try to reuse the cell handler mechanism, so that symbols and keywords work automatically for your fixture.

To iterate through a list of Parse objects, use the More property. Here is an example from Fixture source code:

```
1    private void AddRowToTable(Parse cells, Parse rows)
2    {
3      rows.Last.More = new Parse("tr", null, cells, null);
4    }
```

Use the Parts property to traverse child elements of rows or tables. Although the property is called Parts, it actually points to the first child element, that is, the first cell in the row, not to a list of cells.

```
1    public virtual void DoRow(Parse row)
2    {
3      DoCells(row.Parts);
4    }
```

Tables are represented by linked lists that can change during the test. For example, by changing the value of the More property, you can dynamically append cells and rows to the table during the test. Here is how RowFixture adds surplus rows:

```
1    private void AddRowToTable(Parse cells, Parse rows)
2    {
3      rows.Last.More = new Parse("tr", null, cells, null);
4    }
```

Use the methods Right(Parse p) and Wrong(Parse p, String actualValue) to mark parts of the table as correct or wrong. You can use the Exception (Parse cell, Exception exception) method to signal an exception during processing. Exceptions are handled automatically if you reuse DoCell.

To read cell contents, use the Parse.Text property rather than Parse.Body, as this will strip all HTML tags and give you a pure string. To modify a cell, call Parse.AddToBody. This is how the symbol recall cell handler displays the current symbol value during processing. Consider using Fixture.Gray to format notes and annotations or Fixture.Label to format important messages, to keep your code consistent with other fixtures. For example, here is how RowFixture marks a row as missing:

```
1  private void MarkRowAsMissing(Parse row)
2  {
3      Parse cell = row.Parts;
4      cell.AddToBody(Label("missing"));
5      Wrong(cell);
6  }
```

Stuff to remember

- When tests are hanging and locking resources, you should look for FitServer.exe processes to kill rather than stopping the Java process that runs FitNesse.
- The parse tree represents the test script in memory. Fixtures modify it to display results.
- The Fixture class is the main workflow controller and coordinator for tests.
- Fixture arguments are not accessible to the class constructor so you have to check for them later.
- Symbols and keywords are handled by CellOperation handlers.
- The Accessor interface provides an abstraction that allows us to use methods, interfaces and properties in the same way.
- Most fixtures use the TypeAdapter to convert cell contents into objects. This class looks for a public static Parse method to perform the conversion.
- Use TestRunner.exe to debug fixtures from Visual Studio.

Part IV. Appendices

Formatting text

FitNesse is a wiki, a relatively free-form content management system that allows users to build pages and link them together. Instead of using HTML directly, wikis use a special mark-up syntax. Here is a short summary of the markup symbols:

Markup	Effect
!1	Apply Heading 1 style to the rest of the line
!2	Apply Heading 2 style to the rest of the line
!3	Apply Heading 3 style to the rest of the line
!c	Align to centre
----	Horizontal line (four or more dashes)
!img url	Display image from the URL url
!img-l url	Display image, left aligned
!img-r url	Display image, right aligned
'''text'''	Bold (three single quotes enclosing text on each side).
''text''	Italics (two single quotes enclosing text on each side).
#	Comment – ignore the rest of the line
!include Page Link	Include another page as a component
!include -c Page Link	Include another page with the block collapsed by default
!* Block name block content *!	Collapsible block, open by default
!*> Block name block content *!	Collapsible block, closed by default (note > after the * in the first line)
!contents	Show links to all subpages
!contents -R	Show links to all subpages and their subpages (recursively)

[[label][url]]	Explicit link: can be used to create links that FitNesse does not recognise (if the word is not in CamelCase), or to change the default label for the link.
.PageName	Link to the top level page (prefixed by a dot)
<PageName	Link to the parent-level page (< in front)
>PageName	Link to the child-level page (> in front)
{{{ block content }}}	Preformatted text (does not prevent formatting links and special characters)
!- block content -!	No formatting (can be inline or multi-line). Prevents all formatting. Can be used to include HTML code or put multi-line content into table cells.

See http://FitNesse.org/FitNesse.MarkupLanguageReference for more detailed reference information on the wiki markup language of FitNesse.

Appendix B.

Test smells

Here is a brief summary of things you should watch out for in your tests, and ideas on how to fix them. Use this page as a check list to see whether it is time to do some housekeeping on your FitNesse pages.

- Repetitive values in table cells, especially if the whole column is the same. See section *"Replace repetitive values with arguments"* on page 43.
- Lot of similar tests with minor differences in workflow. See sidebar *"Don't test workflow, get to business rules"* on page 78.
- Test pages containing complex tables that are not really important for the particular test (often just used to set up the stage for the test, and copied from an different test page). See section *"Remove irrelevant information"* on page 77.
- Tests that don't belong to a test suite but have the same setup as other tests. See section *"Group related tests into test suites"* on page 71.
- Parts of test pages or even complete pages used as setup for other tests. Tests that are extensions of other tests. See section *"Beware of test extensions"* on page 99.
- Fixtures implementing a business interface or providing setters and getters to properties of a complex business object. See sidebar *"Don't reimplement business interfaces"* on page 145.
- Tests that reflect the way code was written (you can spot them by looking if tables are too detailed or step-oriented when they should really be focused on higher-level activities). See tip *"Think about the intention, not the implementation"* on page 30.
- Test suites with a mix of quick and slow tests. See section *"Don't mix quick and slow tests"* on page 111.
- Tests that fail intermittently even though you haven't changed the code (especially those that depend on external systems, or on the order of execution). See sidebar *"Beware of unstable tests"* on page 146.
- Fixture methods that mostly deal with conversion from table content into business types. See section *"Avoid conversions by supporting custom data types"* on page 159.

Appendix C.

Resources

Here are some books and online resources that you will find of interest.

Books

[1] Kent Beck. Copyright © 2000. Addison-Wesley Publishing Company. *Extreme Programming Explained: Embrace Change*. 0201616416.

[2] Rick Mugridge and Ward Cunningham. Copyright © 2005. Prentice Hall PTR. *Fit for Developing Software: Framework for Integrated Tests*. 978-0321269348.

[3] Mary Poppendieck and Tom Poppendieck. Copyright © 2006. Addison-Wesley Publishing Company. *Implementing Lean Software Development: From Concept to Cash*. 0321437381.

[4] Kent Beck and Cynthia Andres. Copyright © 2004. Addison-Wesley Publishing Company. *Extreme Programming Explained: Embrace Change*. Second Edition. 0321278658.

[5] Michael Feathers. Copyright © 2004. Prentice Hall. *Working Effectively with Legacy Code*. 0131177052.

[6] Martin Fowler. Copyright © 1999. Addison-Wesley Publishing Company. *Refactoring: Improving the Design of Existing Code*. 0201485672.

[7] Mike Cohn. Copyright © 2004. Addison-Wesley Professional. *User Stories Applied: For Agile Software Development*. 978-0321205681.

[8] Shigeo Shingo. Copyright © 1986. Productivity Press. *Zero Quality Control: Source Inspection and the Poka-Yoke System*. 0915299070.

[9] Ron Jeffries, Ann Anderson, and Chet Hendrickson. Copyright © 2002. Addison-Wesley Professional. *Extreme Programming Installed*. 0201745763.

Web sites

Main FitNesse site

Contains the official user guide (Java version), full reference of the wiki mark-up syntax and further examples: http://www.FitNesse.org. Be sure you view http://FitNesse.org/FitNesse.DotNet.SuiteAcceptanceTests, the page with online acceptance tests for the .NET implementation. Browse through it to find new features and find out how to use them.

FIT web site

Contains additional documentation, FAQ and more examples: http://fit.c2.com/

FitNesse Yahoo group

Online discussion forum, mailing list and file repository for all things related to FitNesse:http://tech.groups.yahoo.com/group/fitnesse/. This is where to ask for help.

FitNesse.NET SVN repository

Browse the latest source code for FitNesse.NET integration and see how things really work: http://fitnessedotnet.svn.sourceforge.net/svnroot/fitnessedotnet/trunk/

Examples from Fit for Developing Software [2] ported to .NET

http://www.vlagsma.com/fitnesse/

FitNesse.NET plans

Mike Stockdale's page on FitNesse.NET development: http://www.syterra.com/FitnesseDotNet.html

FitLibrary homepage

http://fitlibrary.sourceforge.net/

Agile testing resources

http://testing.com/agile/

Blogs with good articles on FitNesse.NET

The Quest For Software++

my blog: http://gojko.net

Cory Foy

http://www.cornetdesign.com/

The Shade Tree Developer

Jeremy D. Miller: http://codebetter.com/blogs/jeremy.miller/

Ruslan Trifonov

http://xman892.blogspot.com/

Google testing blog

http://googletesting.blogspot.com/

Test-obsessed

http://www.testobsessed.com/

Successful Software

James Shore: http://www.jamesshore.com/Blog

Articles

Martin Fowler: Continous Integration

http://www.martinfowler.com/articles/continuousIntegration.html

James Carr: TDD Anti-Patterns

http://blog.james-carr.org/?p=44

Michael Feathers: A Set of Unit Testing Rules

http://www.artima.com/weblogs/viewpost.jsp?thread=126923

Michael Feathers: Working Effectively With Legacy Code

http://www.objectmentor.com/resources/
articles/WorkingEffectivelyWithLegacyCode.pdf

John R. Grout, and Brian T. Downs: A Brief Tutorial on Mistake-proofing, Poka-Yoke, and ZQC

http://csob.berry.edu/faculty/jgrout/tutorial.html

Robert C. Martin: Three rules of TDD

http://butunclebob.com/ArticleS.UncleBob.TheThreeRulesOfTdd:

Jeffrey Palermo: Integrating FitNesse and CC.Net

http://fitnesse.codebetter.com/blogs/jeffrey.palermo/
archive/2005/09/13/131914.aspx

Michael Feathers: Pitching a FIT

http://www.artima.com/weblogs/viewpost.jsp?thread=67373

Sean Shubin: Test First Guidelines

http://www.xprogramming.com/xpmag/testFirstGuidelines.htm

Dan North: Introducing Behaviour-Driven Development

http://dannorth.net/introducing-bdd/

James Shore: A vision for FIT

http://www.jamesshore.com/Blog/A-Vision-For-Fit.html

James Shore: How I use FIT

http://www.jamesshore.com/Blog/How-I-Use-Fit.html

Steve Donie, Using version control with FitNesse, revisited

http://donie.homeip.net:8080/pebble/
Steve/2007/03/02/1172854856750.html

Video presentations and slides

Mary Poppendieck, Competing on the basis of Speed

http://video.google.com/videoplay?docid=-5105910452864283694

Rick Mugridge, Doubling the value of automated tests

http://video.google.co.uk/videoplay?docid=-7227306990557696708 and http://www.rimuresearch.com/ RickMugridgeGoogleConference.pdf

Valtech: FIT/FitNesse - an agile journey

http://www.valtech-tv.com/permalink/2167/fitfitnesse-an-agile-journey-part-i.aspx and http://www.valtech-tv.com/perma-link/2168/fitfitnesse-an-agile-journey-part-ii.aspx

Elliotte Rusty Harold, Test driven web applications with FitNesse

http://www.cafeaulait.org/slides/sdbestpractices2006/fitnesse/:

J.B.Rasinberger: Customer Friendly Testing

http://www.diasparsoftware.com/ presentations/CustomerFriendlyTesting/www/img0.html:

Promising tools

There's a whole new generation of tools emerging that should take concepts laid out by FIT and FitNesse to the next level. Some of these are Java-centric, but they may prove to be very helpful. Watch out for them in the future:

ZiBreve

Rick Mugridge is working on *ZiBrieve,* an Eclipse-like IDE for story tests, with WYSIWYG editing and support for refactoring, with the intention of making it easier to manage large suites of story tests: http://www.zibreve.com/.

StoryTeller

Jeremy D. Miller is working on *StoryTeller,* which promises to provide an effective way to write and manage tests and support an acceptance test driven development strategy with tagging, good integration with source control systems and automated build tools, while keeping compatibility with FIT/FitNesse tests: http://storyteller.tigris.org.

Profit

The people at ThoughtWorks are working on *Profit*, a tool that converts FIT tests to code to enable easy refactoring: http://sourceforge.net/projects/profit.

FitNesse from TestDriven.Net

Jay Flowers is working on a plugin for *TestDriven.Net*, which starts FitNesse tests from Visual Studio: http://jayflowers.com/Word-Press/?p=157.

AspFitNesse

Owen Evans is working on a .NET version of FitNesse, which will not require Java to run: http://sourceforge.net/projects/aspfitnesse.

FitNesse Nant Tasks

Jeff Parker is working on a set of NAnt tasks for FitNesse integration: http://sourceforge.net/projects/fnessenanttasks/

Concordion

Concordion is an opensource framework for acceptance testing in plain English. Instead of tables, like FitNesse, it uses HTML markup in sentences to map the English document to test fixtures. http://www.concordion.org

Appendix D.

Source code

This appendix contains full source code of all examples used in the book. We have built some examples gradually throughout the book, so some files contain several versions of test classes. In those cases, you will see different stages put into namespaces such as FirstTry, SecondTry etc. You can also download all these files from http://gojko.net/fitnesse.

C# Classes

HelloWorld/HelloWorld.cs

```
1   namespace HelloWorld
2   {
3       public class OurFirstTest : fit.ColumnFixture
4       {
5           public string string1;
6           public string string2;
7           public string Concatenate()
8           {
9               return string1 + " " + string2;
10          }
11      }
12  }
```

SeleniumTest/Console.cs

```
1   using System;
2   using Selenium;
3   namespace SeleniumTest
4   {
5       class Console
6       {
7           static void Main(string[] args)
8           {
9               ISelenium sel = new DefaultSelenium("localhost",
10              4444, "*iehta", "http://www.google.com");
11              sel.Start();
12              sel.Open("http://www.google.com/");
13              sel.Type("q", "FitNesse");
14              sel.Click("btnG");
```

```
15        sel.WaitForPageToLoad("3000");
16      }
17    }
18  }
```

Tristan/src/IDraw.cs

```
1   using System;
2   using System.Collections.Generic;
3   using System.Text;
4
5   namespace Tristan
6   {
7     public interface IDraw
8     {
9       DateTime DrawDate { get; }
10      bool IsOpen { get; }
11      decimal TotalPoolSize { get;}
12
13      ITicket[] Tickets { get;}
14      void AddTicket(ITicket ticket);
15    }
16  }
```

Tristan/src/IDrawManager.cs

```
1   using System;
2   using System.Collections.Generic;
3   using System.Text;
4
5   namespace Tristan
6   {
7     public class DrawNotOpenException : ApplicationException
8     {
9       public DrawNotOpenException()
10        : base("Draw is closed")
11      {
12      }
13    }
14    interface IDrawManager
15    {
16      IDraw GetDraw(DateTime date);
17      IDraw CreateDraw(DateTime drawDate);
18      void PurchaseTicket(DateTime drawDate, int playerId,
19        int[] numbers, decimal value);
20      void SettleDraw(DateTime drawDate, int[] results);
21      decimal OperatorDeductionFactor { get; }
22      List<ITicket> GetOpenTickets(int playerId);
```

```
23        List<ITicket> GetTickets(DateTime drawDate, int playerId);
24    }
25 }
```

Tristan/src/IPlayerInfo.cs

```
1  using System;
2  using System.Collections.Generic;
3  using System.Text;
4
5  namespace Tristan
6  {
7    public interface IPlayerInfo
8    {
9      string Name { get;}
10     string Address { get;}
11     string City { get;}
12     string PostCode { get;}
13     string Country { get;}
14     string Username { get;}
15     decimal Balance { get;}
16     int PlayerId { get;}
17     bool IsVerified { get;}
18   }
19 }
```

Tristan/src/IPlayerManager.cs

```
1  using System;
2  using System.Collections.Generic;
3  using System.Text;
4
5  namespace Tristan
6  {
7    public class UnknownPlayerException : ApplicationException
8    {
9      public UnknownPlayerException() : base("Unknown user") { }
10   }
11   public class InvalidPasswordException: ApplicationException
12   {
13     public InvalidPasswordException():base("Invalid password"){}
14   }
15   public class DuplicateUsernameException : ApplicationException
16   {
17     public DuplicateUsernameException() : base("Duplicate username") { }
18   }
19   public class NotEnoughFundsException : ApplicationException
20   {
```

```
21      public NotEnoughFundsException() : base("Not enough funds") { }
22    }
23    public class TransactionDeclinedException : ApplicationException
24    {
25      public TransactionDeclinedException() : base("Transaction declined")
{ }
26    }
27
28    public interface IPlayerManager
29    {
30      int RegisterPlayer(IPlayerRegistrationInfo p);
31      IPlayerInfo GetPlayer(int id);
32      IPlayerInfo GetPlayer(String username);
33      int LogIn(String username, String password);
34      void AdjustBalance(int playerId, decimal amount);
35      void DepositWithCard(int playerId, String cardNumber,
36        String expiryDate, decimal amount);
37    }
38  }
```

Tristan/src/IPlayerRegistrationInfo.cs

```
1    using System;
2    using System.Collections.Generic;
3    using System.Text;
4
5    namespace Tristan
6    {
7      public interface IPlayerRegistrationInfo
8      {
9        string Name { get;}
10       string Address { get;}
11       string City { get;}
12       string PostCode { get;}
13       string Country { get;}
14       string Username { get;}
15       string Password { get;}
16     }
17   }
```

Tristan/src/ITicket.cs

```
1    using System;
2    using System.Collections.Generic;
3    using System.Text;
4
5    namespace Tristan
6    {
```

```
7    public interface ITicket
8    {
9      int[] Numbers { get;}
10     IPlayerInfo Holder { get;}
11     decimal Value {get;}
12     bool IsOpen { get;}
13     decimal Winnings { get; }
14     DateTime draw { get; }
15   }
16 }
```

Tristan/src/InitialWinningsCalculator.cs

```
1    namespace Tristan
2    {
3      public class WinningsCalculator
4      {
5        public int GetPoolPercentage(int combination)
6        {
7          throw new Exception("Not implemented");
8        }
9        public decimal GetPrizePool(int combination, decimal payoutPool)
10       {
11         throw new Exception("Not implemented");
12       }
13     }
14 }
```

Tristan/src/WinningsCalculator.cs

```
1    namespace Tristan
2    {
3      public class WinningsCalculator
4      {
5        public int GetPoolPercentage(int combination)
6        {
7          switch(combination) {
8            case 6: return 68;
9            case 5: return 10;
10           case 4: return 10;
11           case 3: return 12;
12           default: return 0;
13         }
14       }
15       public decimal GetPrizePool(int combination, decimal payoutPool)
16       {
17         return payoutPool * GetPoolPercentage(combination) / 100;
18       }
```

```
19    }
20  }
```

Tristan/src/inproc/Draw.cs

```
1    using System;
2    using System.Collections.Generic;
3    using System.Text;
4    using Tristan;
5    namespace Tristan.inproc
6    {
7      class Draw:IDraw
8      {
9        public Draw(DateTime drawDate)
10       {
11         this._totalSize = 0;
12         this._drawDate = drawDate;
13         this._isOpen = true;
14         this._tickets = new List<ITicket>();
15       }
16       private DateTime _drawDate;
17       public DateTime DrawDate
18       {
19         get { return _drawDate; }
20       }
21       private bool _isOpen;
22       public bool IsOpen
23       {
24         get { return _isOpen; }
25         set { _isOpen = value; }
26       }
27       private decimal _totalSize;
28       public decimal TotalPoolSize
29       {
30         get { return _totalSize; }
31       }
32       private List<ITicket> _tickets;
33       public ITicket[] Tickets
34       {
35         get { return _tickets.ToArray();}
36       }
37       public void AddTicket(ITicket ticket)
38       {
39         _tickets.Add(ticket);
40         _totalSize += ticket.Value;
41       }
42     }
43  }
```

Tristan/src/inproc/DrawManager.cs

```
1    using System;
2    using System.Collections.Generic;
3    using System.Text;
4    using Tristan;
5    namespace Tristan.inproc
6    {
7      public class DrawManager : IDrawManager
8      {
9        private Dictionary<DateTime, Draw> _draws=new
   Dictionary<DateTime,Draw>();
10       private IPlayerManager _playerManager;
11       public DrawManager(IPlayerManager playerMgr)
12       {
13         this._playerManager = playerMgr;
14       }
15       public IDraw GetDraw(DateTime date)
16       {
17         return _draws[date];
18       }
19       public IDraw CreateDraw(DateTime drawDate)
20       {
21         Draw d = new Draw(drawDate);
22         _draws[drawDate] = d;
23         return d;
24       }
25       public void PurchaseTicket(DateTime drawDate, int playerId, int[]
   numbers, decimal value)
26       {
27         if (!_draws.ContainsKey(drawDate))
28           throw new DrawNotOpenException();
29         Draw d = _draws[drawDate];
30         IPlayerInfo player=_playerManager.GetPlayer(playerId);
31         _playerManager.AdjustBalance(playerId, -1 * value);
32         d.AddTicket(new Ticket(player,drawDate, numbers,value));
33       }
34       private int CountCommonElements(int[] array1, int[] array2)
35       {
36         int common = 0;
37         foreach (int i in array1)
38           foreach (int j in array2)
39             if (i == j) common++;
40         return common;
41       }
42       public void SettleDraw(DateTime drawDate, int[] results)
43       {
44         WinningsCalculator wc = new WinningsCalculator();
```

```
45        Draw d = _draws[drawDate];
46        d.IsOpen = false;
47        Dictionary<int, List<Ticket>>
ticketCategories=SplitTicketsIntoCategories(results, d);
48        for (int i = 0; i <= results.Length; i++)
49        {
50          decimal prizePool=wc.GetPrizePool(i, d.TotalPoolSize * (1-
OperatorDeductionFactor));
51          foreach (Ticket t in ticketCategories[i])
52          {
53            t.IsOpen = false;
54            if (prizePool > 0)
55            {
56              decimal totalTicketValue =
GetTotalTicketValue(ticketCategories[i]);
57              t.Winnings = t.Value * prizePool / totalTicketValue;
58              _playerManager.AdjustBalance(t.Holder.PlayerId,
59                t.Winnings);
60            }
61          }
62        }
63      }
64
65      private static decimal GetTotalTicketValue(List<Ticket> tickets)
66      {
67        decimal totalTicketValue = 0;
68        foreach (Ticket t in tickets)
69          totalTicketValue += t.Value;
70        return totalTicketValue;
71      }
72      public decimal OperatorDeductionFactor { get { return 0.5m; } }
73      private Dictionary<int, List<Ticket>>
SplitTicketsIntoCategories(int[] results, Draw d)
74      {
75        Dictionary<int, List<Ticket>> ticketcategories = new
Dictionary<int, List<Ticket>>();
76        for (int i = 0; i <= results.Length; i++)
77          ticketcategories[i] = new List<Ticket>();
78        foreach (Ticket t in d.Tickets)
79        {
80          int c = CountCommonElements(t.Numbers, results);
81          ticketcategories[c].Add(t);
82        }
83        return ticketcategories;
84      }
85
86
87      public List<ITicket> GetOpenTickets(int playerId)
88      {
```

```
89          List<ITicket> tickets = new List<ITicket>();
90          foreach (Draw d in _draws.Values)
91          {
92            if (d.IsOpen){
93              tickets.AddRange(GetTickets(d.DrawDate,playerId));
94            }
95          }
96          return tickets;
97        }
98        public List<ITicket> GetTickets(DateTime drawDate, int playerId)
99        {
100         List<ITicket> tickets = new List<ITicket>();
101         foreach (Ticket t in _draws[drawDate].Tickets)
102         {
103           if (t.Holder.PlayerId == playerId)
104             tickets.Add(t);
105         }
106         return tickets;
107       }
108  }
109 }
```

Tristan/src/inproc/PlayerInfo.cs

```
1   using System;
2   using System.Collections.Generic;
3   using System.Text;
4   using Tristan;
5   namespace Tristan.inproc
6   {
7     public class PlayerInfo:IPlayerInfo
8     {
9       private static int nextId=1;
10      public PlayerInfo(IPlayerRegistrationInfo reg)
11      {
12        this._address = reg.Address;
13        this._balance = 0;
14        this._city = reg.City;
15        this._country = reg.Country;
16        this._name = reg.Name;
17        this._postcode = reg.PostCode;
18        this._playerId = nextId++;
19        this._username = reg.Username;
20        this._password = reg.Password;
21      }
22
23      private string _password;
24      internal string Password { get { return _password; } }
```

```
25
26       private string _name;
27       public string Name
28       {
29         get { return _name; }
30         set { _name = value; }
31       }
32
33       private string _address;
34       public string Address
35       {
36         get { return _address; }
37         set { _address = value; }
38       }
39
40       private string _city;
41       public string City
42       {
43         get { return _city; }
44         set { _city = value; }
45       }
46
47       private string _postcode;
48       public string PostCode
49       {
50         get { return _postcode; }
51         set { _postcode = value; }
52       }
53       private string _country;
54       public string Country
55       {
56         get { return _country;  }
57         set { _country = value; }
58       }
59
60       private string _username;
61       public string Username
62       {
63         get { return _username; }
64         set { _username = value; }
65       }
66
67       private decimal _balance;
68       public decimal Balance
69       {
70         get { return _balance; }
71         set { _balance = value; }
72       }
73       private int _playerId;
```

```
74     public int PlayerId
75     {
76       get { return _playerId; }
77       set { _playerId = value; }
78     }
79     private bool _verified;
80     public bool IsVerified {
81       get { return _verified; }
82       set { _verified = value; }
83     }
84   }
85 }
```

Tristan/src/inproc/PlayerManager.cs

```
1    using System;
2    using System.Collections.Generic;
3    using System.Text;
4    using Tristan;
5    namespace Tristan.inproc
6    {
7      public class PlayerManager:IPlayerManager
8      {
9        private Dictionary<int,PlayerInfo> _players = new
     Dictionary<int,PlayerInfo>();
10       private Dictionary<string, PlayerInfo> _playersByName = new
     Dictionary<string, PlayerInfo>();
11       public PlayerManager() { }
12       public int RegisterPlayer(IPlayerRegistrationInfo p)
13       {
14         if (_playersByName.ContainsKey(p.Username)) throw new
     DuplicateUsernameException();
15         PlayerInfo np = new PlayerInfo(p);
16         _players.Add(np.PlayerId, np);
17         _playersByName.Add(np.Username, np);
18         return np.PlayerId;
19       }
20
21       public IPlayerInfo GetPlayer(int id)
22       {
23         return _players[id];
24       }
25       public IPlayerInfo GetPlayer(String username)
26       {
27         if (!_playersByName.ContainsKey(username)) throw new
     UnknownPlayerException();
28         PlayerInfo pi = _playersByName[username];
29         return pi;
```

```
30        }
31
32        public int LogIn(String username, String password)
33        {
34            if (!_playersByName.ContainsKey(username)) throw new
     UnknownPlayerException();
35            PlayerInfo pi = _playersByName[username];
36            if (password.Equals(pi.Password)) return pi.PlayerId;
37            throw new InvalidPasswordException();
38        }
39
40        public void AdjustBalance(int playerId, decimal amount)
41        {
42          PlayerInfo pi = _players[playerId];
43          if (amount < 0 && pi.Balance < (-1 * amount))
44            throw new NotEnoughFundsException();
45          pi.Balance += amount;
46        }
47
48        public void DepositWithCard(int playerId, string cardNumber, string
     expiryDate, decimal amount)
49        {
50          if (cardNumber.EndsWith("2"))
51            throw new TransactionDeclinedException();
52          PlayerInfo pi = _players[playerId];
53          pi.Balance += amount;
54        }
55      }
56 }
```

Tristan/src/inproc/PlayerRegistrationInfo.cs

```
1    using System;
2    using System.Collections.Generic;
3    using System.Text;
4    using Tristan.Test;
5    namespace Tristan.inproc
6    {
7      public class PlayerRegistrationInfo: IPlayerRegistrationInfo
8      {
9        private string _name;
10       public string Name { get { return _name; } set { _name = value; } }
11
12       private string _address;
13       public string Address { get { return _address; } set { _address =
     value; } }
14
15       private string _city;
```

```
16      public string City { get { return _city; } set { _city = value; } }
17
18      private string _postCode;
19      public string PostCode { get { return _postCode; } set { _postCode =
value; } }
20
21      private string _country;
22      public string Country { get { return _country; } set { _country =
value; } }
23
24      private string _username;
25      public string Username { get { return _username; } set { _username =
value; } }
26
27      private string _password;
28      public string Password { get { return _password; } set { _password =
value; } }
29    }
30  }
```

Tristan/src/inproc/Ticket.cs

```
1    using System;
2    using System.Collections.Generic;
3    using System.Text;
4
5    namespace Tristan.inproc
6    {
7      class Ticket:ITicket
8      {
9        public Ticket(IPlayerInfo holder, DateTime draw, int[] numbers,
decimal value)
10       {
11         _numbers = new int[numbers.Length];
12         System.Array.Copy(numbers, _numbers, numbers.Length);
13         _holder = holder;
14         _value = value;
15         _open = true;
16         _winnings = 0;
17         _drawDate = draw;
18       }
19       private int[] _numbers;
20       public int[] Numbers
21       {
22         get { return _numbers; }
23       }
24
25       private IPlayerInfo _holder;
```

```
26      public IPlayerInfo Holder
27      {
28        get { return _holder; }
29      }
30      private decimal _value;
31      public decimal Value
32      {
33        get { return _value; }
34      }
35
36      private bool _open;
37      public bool IsOpen
38      {
39        get { return _open; }
40        set { _open = value; }
41      }
42      private decimal _winnings;
43      public decimal Winnings
44      {
45        get { return _winnings; }
46        set { _winnings = value; }
47      }
48      private DateTime _drawDate;
49      public DateTime draw
50      {
51        get { return _drawDate; }
52      }
53    }
54  }
```

Tristan/test/PayoutTable.cs

```
1   namespace Tristan.Test
2   {
3     public class PayoutTable:fit.ColumnFixture
4     {
5       private WinningsCalculator wc=new WinningsCalculator();
6       public int winningCombination;
7       public decimal payoutPool;
8       public int PoolPercentage()
9       {
10        return wc.GetPoolPercentage(winningCombination);
11      }
12      public decimal PrizePool()
13      {
14        return wc.GetPrizePool(winningCombination, payoutPool);
15      }
16    }
```

```
17  }
```

Tristan/test/PlayerRegistration.cs

```
1   using fit;
2   using Tristan.inproc;
3   using System;
4   namespace Tristan.Test
5   {
6     public class SetUpTestEnvironment : Fixture
7     {
8       internal static IPlayerManager playerManager;
9       public SetUpTestEnvironment()
10      {
11        playerManager = new PlayerManager();
12      }
13    }
14  }
15  namespace Tristan.Test.FirstTry
16  {
17    public class PlayerRegisters : ColumnFixture
18    {
19      public string Username;
20      public string Password;
21      public int NewPlayerId()
22      {
23        PlayerRegistrationInfo reg = new PlayerRegistrationInfo();
24        reg.Username = Username;
25        reg.Password = Password;
26        return SetUpTestEnvironment.playerManager.RegisterPlayer(reg);
27      }
28    }
29    public class CheckStoredDetails : ColumnFixture
30    {
31      public int PlayerId;
32      public string Username
33      {
34        get
35        {
36          return SetUpTestEnvironment.playerManager.
37            GetPlayer(PlayerId).Username;
38        }
39      }
40      public decimal Balance
41      {
42        get
43        {
44          return SetUpTestEnvironment.playerManager.
```

```
45            GetPlayer(PlayerId).Balance;
46        }
47      }
48    }
49    public class CheckLogIn:ColumnFixture{
50      public string Username;
51      public string Password;
52      public bool CanLogIn()
53      {
54        try
55        {
56          SetUpTestEnvironment.playerManager.LogIn(Username, Password);
57          return true;
58        }
59        catch (ApplicationException)
60        {
61          return false;
62        }
63      }
64    }
65  }
66  namespace Tristan.Test.SecondTry
67  {
68    public class PlayerRegisters : ColumnFixture
69    {
70      public class ExtendedPlayerRegistrationInfo: PlayerRegistrationInfo
71      {
72        public int NewPlayerId()
73        {
74          return SetUpTestEnvironment.playerManager.RegisterPlayer(this);
75        }
76      }
77      private ExtendedPlayerRegistrationInfo to =
78        new ExtendedPlayerRegistrationInfo();
79      public override object  GetTargetObject()
80      {
81          return to;
82      }
83    }
84    public class CheckStoredDetailsFor : ColumnFixture
85    {
86      public override object GetTargetObject()
87      {
88        int newid=(int)Fixture.Recall(Args[0]);
89        return SetUpTestEnvironment.playerManager.GetPlayer(newid);
90      }
91    }
92    public class CheckLogIn : ColumnFixture
93    {
```

```
94      public string Username;
95      public string Password;
96      public int LoggedInAsPlayerId()
97      {
98        return SetUpTestEnvironment.playerManager.
99          LogIn(Username, Password);
100     }
101   }
102 }
```

Tristan/test/PurchaseTicket.cs

```
1    using System;
2    using System.Collections.Generic;
3    using System.Text;
4    using Tristan.inproc;
5    using fit;
6    namespace Tristan.Test.PurchaseTicket
7    {
8      public class SetUpTestEnvironment : ColumnFixture
9      {
10       internal static IPlayerManager playerManager;
11       internal static IDrawManager drawManager;
12       public SetUpTestEnvironment()
13       {
14         playerManager = new PlayerManager();
15         drawManager = new DrawManager(playerManager);
16       }
17       public DateTime CreateDraw {
18         set
19         {
20           drawManager.CreateDraw(value);
21         }
22       }
23     }
24     public class PlayerRegisters : ColumnFixture
25     {
26       public class ExtendedPlayerRegistrationInfo:
27         PlayerRegistrationInfo
28       {
29         public int NewPlayerId()
30         {
31           return SetUpTestEnvironment.playerManager.
32             RegisterPlayer(this);
33         }
34       }
35       private ExtendedPlayerRegistrationInfo to =
36         new ExtendedPlayerRegistrationInfo();
```

```
37      public override object GetTargetObject()
38      {
39        return to;
40      }
41    }
42    public class PurchaseTicket : fitlibrary.DoFixture
43    {
44      public void PlayerDepositsDollarsWithCardAndExpiryDate(
45        string username, decimal amount, string card, string expiry)
46      {
47        int pid = SetUpTestEnvironment.playerManager.
48                        GetPlayer(username).PlayerId;
49        SetUpTestEnvironment.playerManager.DepositWithCard(
50          pid, card, expiry, amount);
51      }
52      public bool PlayerHasDollars(String username, decimal amount)
53      {
54        return (SetUpTestEnvironment.playerManager.
55            GetPlayer(username).Balance == amount);
56      }
57      public void PlayerBuysATicketWithNumbersForDrawOn(
58        string username, int[] numbers, DateTime date)
59      {
60        PlayerBuysTicketsWithNumbersForDrawOn(
61          username, 1, numbers, date);
62      }
63      public void PlayerBuysTicketsWithNumbersForDrawOn(
64        string username, int tickets, int[] numbers, DateTime date)
65      {
66        int pid = SetUpTestEnvironment.playerManager.
67                        GetPlayer(username).PlayerId;
68        SetUpTestEnvironment.drawManager.PurchaseTicket(
69          date, pid, numbers, 10*tickets);
70      }
71      public bool PoolValueForDrawOnIsDollars(DateTime date,
72                        decimal amount)
73      {
74        return SetUpTestEnvironment.drawManager.GetDraw(date).
75                    TotalPoolSize == amount;
76      }
77      private static bool CompareArrays(int[] sorted1, int[] unsorted2)
78      {
79        if (sorted1.Length != unsorted2.Length) return false;
80        Array.Sort(unsorted2);
81        for (int i = 0; i < sorted1.Length; i++)
82        {
83          if (sorted1[i] != unsorted2[i]) return false;
84        }
85        return true;
```

```
86         }
87       public bool
88           TicketWithNumbersForDollarsIsRegisteredForPlayerForDrawOn(
89         int[] numbers, decimal amount, string username, DateTime draw)
90       {
91         ITicket[] tck = SetUpTestEnvironment.
92           drawManager.GetDraw(draw).Tickets;
93         Array.Sort(numbers);
94         foreach (ITicket ticket in tck)
95         {
96           if (CompareArrays(numbers, ticket.Numbers) &&
97               amount == ticket.Value &&
98               username.Equals(ticket.Holder.Username))
99             return true;
100        }
101        return false;
102      }
103      public decimal PoolValueForDrawOnIs(DateTime date)
104      {
105          return SetUpTestEnvironment.drawManager.
106            GetDraw(date).TotalPoolSize;
107      }
108      public decimal AccountBalanceFor(String username)
109      {
110        return SetUpTestEnvironment.playerManager.
111          GetPlayer(username).Balance;
112      }
113    }
114 }
```

Tristan/test/ReviewTickets.cs

```
1    using System;
2    using System.Collections.Generic;
3    using System.Text;
4    using Tristan;
5    using Tristan.inproc;
6    using fit;
7    namespace Tristan.Test
8    {
9      public class ReviewTickets:fitlibrary.DoFixture
10     {
11       private IDrawManager _drawManager;
12       private IPlayerManager _playerManager;
13       public ReviewTickets()
14       {
15         _playerManager = new PlayerManager();
16         _drawManager = new DrawManager(_playerManager);
```

```
17        }
18        public void DrawOnIsOpen(DateTime drawDate)
19        {
20          _drawManager.CreateDraw(drawDate);
21        }
22        public void PlayerOpensAccountWithDollars(String player, decimal
   balance)
23        {
24          PlayerRegistrationInfo p = new PlayerRegistrationInfo();
25          p.Username = player; p.Name = player;
26          p.Password = "XXXXXX";
27          // define other mandatory properties
28          int playerId = _playerManager.RegisterPlayer(p);
29          _playerManager.AdjustBalance(playerId, balance);
30        }
31        public void PlayerBuysATicketWithNumbersForDrawOn(
32          string username, int[] numbers, DateTime date)
33        {
34          PlayerBuysTicketsWithNumbersForDrawOn(username, 1, numbers, date);
35        }
36
37        public void PlayerBuysTicketsWithNumbersForDrawOn(
38          string username, int tickets, int[] numbers, DateTime date)
39        {
40          int pid = _playerManager.GetPlayer(username).PlayerId;
41          _drawManager.PurchaseTicket(date, pid, numbers, 10 * tickets);
42        }
43        public IList<ITicket> PlayerListsOpenTickets(String player)
44        {
45          return _drawManager.GetOpenTickets(
46            _playerManager.GetPlayer(player).PlayerId);
47        }
48        public IList<ITicket> PlayerListsTicketsForDrawOn(
49          String player, DateTime date)
50        {
51          return _drawManager.GetTickets(
52            date,_playerManager.GetPlayer(player).PlayerId);
53        }
54        public void NumbersAreDrawnOn(int[] numbers, DateTime date)
55        {
56          _drawManager.SettleDraw(date, numbers);
57        }
58      }
59      public class ReviewTicketsWithRowFixture : fitlibrary.DoFixture
60      {
61        private IDrawManager _drawManager;
62        private IPlayerManager _playerManager;
63        public ReviewTicketsWithRowFixture()
64        {
```

```
65        _playerManager = new PlayerManager();
66        _drawManager = new DrawManager(_playerManager);
67      }
68      public void DrawOnIsOpen(DateTime drawDate)
69      {
70        _drawManager.CreateDraw(drawDate);
71      }
72      public void PlayerOpensAccountWithDollars(
73        String player, decimal balance){
74        PlayerRegistrationInfo p = new PlayerRegistrationInfo();
75        p.Username = player; p.Name = player;
76        p.Password = "XXXXXX";
77        // define other mandatory properties
78        int playerId = _playerManager.RegisterPlayer(p);
79        _playerManager.AdjustBalance(playerId, balance);
80      }
81      public void PlayerBuysATicketWithNumbersForDrawOn(
82        string username, int[] numbers, DateTime date)
83      {
84        PlayerBuysTicketsWithNumbersForDrawOn(
85          username, 1, numbers, date);
86      }
87
88      public void PlayerBuysTicketsWithNumbersForDrawOn(
89        string username, int tickets, int[] numbers, DateTime date)
90      {
91        int pid = _playerManager.GetPlayer(username).PlayerId;
92        _drawManager.PurchaseTicket(date, pid, numbers, 10 * tickets);
93      }
94      public RowFixture PlayerListsOpenTickets(String player)
95      {
96        return new TicketRowFixture(
97          _drawManager.GetOpenTickets(
98            _playerManager.GetPlayer(player).PlayerId));
99      }
100     public RowFixture PlayerListsTicketsForDrawOn(
101       String player, DateTime date)
102     {
103       return new TicketRowFixture(
104         _drawManager.GetTickets(date,
105           _playerManager.GetPlayer(player).PlayerId));
106     }
107     public void NumbersAreDrawnOn(int[] numbers, DateTime date)
108     {
109       _drawManager.SettleDraw(date, numbers);
110     }
111   }
112   public class TicketRowFixture : fit.RowFixture
113   {
```

```
114      private List<ITicket> _internalList;
115      public TicketRowFixture(List<ITicket> tickets)
116      {
117        _internalList = tickets;
118      }
119      public override Type GetTargetClass()
120      {
121        return typeof(ITicket);
122      }
123
124      public override object[] Query()
125      {
126        return _internalList.ToArray();
127      }
128    }
129 }
```

Tristan/test/SetUpTestEnvironment.cs

```
1  using System;
2  using System.Collections.Generic;
3  using System.Text;
4  using fit;
5  using Tristan.inproc;
6  namespace Tristan.Test
7  {
8  }
```

Tristan/test/Settlement.cs

```
1   using System;
2   using System.Collections.Generic;
3   using System.Text;
4   using Tristan;
5   using Tristan.inproc;
6   using fitlibrary;
7   using fit;
8   namespace Tristan.Test.Settlement
9   {
10    internal class BalanceCheckFixture : ColumnFixture
11    {
12      private IPlayerManager _playerManager;
13      public BalanceCheckFixture(IPlayerManager pm)
14      {
15        _playerManager = pm;
16      }
17      public String player;
18      public decimal Balance
```

```
19    {
20      get
21      {
22        return _playerManager.GetPlayer(player).Balance;
23      }
24    }
25  }
26  internal class CreatePlayerFixture : SetUpFixture
27  {
28    private IPlayerManager _playerManager;
29    public CreatePlayerFixture(IPlayerManager pm)
30    {
31      _playerManager = pm;
32    }
33    public void PlayerBalance(String player, decimal balance)
34    {
35      PlayerRegistrationInfo p = new PlayerRegistrationInfo();
36      p.Username = player; p.Name = player;
37      p.Password = "XXXXXX";
38      // define other mandatory properties
39      int playerId = _playerManager.RegisterPlayer(p);
40      _playerManager.AdjustBalance(playerId, balance);
41    }
42  }
43  internal class TicketPurchaseFixture: SetUpFixture
44  {
45    private IDrawManager _drawManager;
46    private DateTime _drawDate;
47    private IPlayerManager _playerManager;
48
49    public TicketPurchaseFixture(IPlayerManager pm, IDrawManager dm,
50      DateTime drawDate)
51    {
52      _drawManager = dm;
53      _playerManager = pm;
54      _drawDate = drawDate;
55    }
56    public void PlayerNumbersValue(String player, int[] numbers, decimal
    value)
57    {
58      _drawManager.PurchaseTicket(_drawDate,
59        _playerManager.GetPlayer(player).PlayerId, numbers, value);
60    }
61  }
62  public class SettlementTest:DoFixture
63  {
64    private IDrawManager drawManager;
65    private IPlayerManager playerManager;
66    private DateTime drawDate;
```

```
67      public SettlementTest()
68      {
69        playerManager = new PlayerManager();
70        drawManager = new DrawManager(playerManager);
71        drawDate = DateTime.Now;
72        drawManager.CreateDraw(drawDate);
73      }
74      public Fixture TicketsInTheDraw()
75      {
76        return new TicketPurchaseFixture(playerManager, drawManager,
   drawDate);
77      }
78      public void DrawResultsAre(int[] numbers)
79      {
80        drawManager.SettleDraw(drawDate, numbers);
81      }
82      public Fixture AccountsAfterTheDraw()
83      {
84        return new BalanceCheckFixture(playerManager);
85      }
86      public Fixture AccountsBeforeTheDraw()
87      {
88        return new CreatePlayerFixture(playerManager);
89      }
90    }
91  }
```

Tristan/test/TotalPoolValue.cs

```
1   using System;
2
3   namespace Tristan.Test
4   {
5     public class PrizeDistributionForPayoutPool:fit.ColumnFixture {
6       private WinningsCalculator wc = new WinningsCalculator();
7       public int winningCombination;
8       public int PoolPercentage()
9       {
10        return wc.GetPoolPercentage(winningCombination);
11      }
12      public decimal? payoutPool;
13      public decimal PrizePool()
14      {
15        if (payoutPool == null) payoutPool = Decimal.Parse(Args[0]);
16        return wc.GetPrizePool(winningCombination, payoutPool.Value);
17      }
18    }
19  }
```

extended/Invoice.cs

```
1    using System;
2    using System.Collections.Generic;
3    using System.Text;
4
5    namespace extended
6    {
7      class TaxCalculator
8      {
9        public decimal GetTax(String code, decimal price)
10       {
11         if (code.StartsWith("B")) return 0;
12         return 0.1m * price;
13       }
14     }
15     public class Invoice:fitnesse.fixtures.TableFixture
16     {
17       protected override void DoStaticTable(int rows)
18       {
19         TaxCalculator tc=new TaxCalculator();
20         decimal totaltax = 0;
21         for (int row = 1; row < rows - 3; row++)
22         {
23           totaltax += tc.GetTax(GetString(row, 1),
24             Decimal.Parse(GetString(row, 2)));
25         }
26         decimal taxintable = Decimal.Parse(GetString(rows - 2, 2));
27         if (taxintable == totaltax)
28           Right(rows - 2, 2);
29         else
30           Wrong(rows - 2, 2, totaltax.ToString());
31       }
32     }
33   }
```

extended/RegExHandler.cs

```
1    using System.Text.RegularExpressions;
2    using fitnesse.handlers;
3    using fit;
4
5    namespace extended
6    {
7      public class RegExHandler: AbstractCellHandler {
8        public override bool Match(string searchString, System.Type type) {
9          return searchString.StartsWith("/") &&
10           searchString.EndsWith("/") &&
```

```
11          typeof(string).Equals(type);
12      }
13      public override bool HandleEvaluate(Fixture fixture, Parse cell,
14          Accessor accessor) {
15        object actualValue=accessor.Get(fixture);
16        if (actualValue == null) return false;
17        Regex expected =new Regex(cell.Text.Substring(1,
cell.Text.Length-2));
18          return expected.IsMatch(actualValue.ToString());
19      }
20    }
21  }
```

webfixture/WebTest.cs

```
1    using System;
2    using System.Collections.Generic;
3    using System.Text;
4    using Selenium;
5
6    namespace webfixture
7    {
8        public class WebTest : fitlibrary.DoFixture
9        {
10           private ISelenium instance;
11           public void StartBrowserWithSeleniumConsoleOnAtPortAndScriptsAt(
12             String browser, String rcServer, int rcPort, String
seleniumURL)
13           {
14               instance = new DefaultSelenium(rcServer,
15                                   rcPort, browser,
seleniumURL);
16               instance.Start();
17           }
18           public void ShutdownBrowser()
19           {
20               instance.Stop();
21           }
22       public static readonly string[] buttonLocators = new String[] {
23       "xpath=//input[@type='submit' and @name='{0}']",
24       "xpath=//input[@type='button' and @name='{0}']",
25       "xpath=//input[@type='submit' and @value='{0}']",
26       "xpath=//input[@type='button' and @value='{0}']",
27       "xpath=//input[@type='submit' and @id='{0}']",
28       "xpath=//input[@type='button' and @id='{0}']"};
29
30           public static readonly string[] selectLocators = new String[] {
```

```
31      "xpath=//select[@name='{0}']",
32      "xpath=//select[@id='{0}']"};
33
34          private String GetLocator(String caption, String[]
   possibleFormats)
35          {
36              foreach (String s in possibleFormats)
37              {
38                  String locator = String.Format(s, caption);
39                  if (instance.IsElementPresent(locator))
40                  {
41                      return locator;
42                  }
43              }
44              throw new ApplicationException(
45              "Cannot find element by " + caption);
46          }
47          public void UserOpensURL(String s)
48          {
49              instance.Open(s);
50          }
51          public static readonly string[] textFieldLocators = new String[]
   {
52      "xpath=//input[@type='text' and @name='{0}']",
53      "xpath=//input[@type='password' and @name='{0}']",
54      "xpath=//textarea[@name='{0}']",
55      "xpath=//input[@type='text' and @id='{0}']",
56      "xpath=//input[@type='password' and @id='{0}']",
57      "xpath=//textarea[@id='{0}']"};
58
59          public void UserTypesIntoField(String what, String where)
60          {
61              instance.Type(GetLocator(
62              where.Replace(" ", ""), textFieldLocators), what);
63          }
64          public void UserClicksOn(String buttonCaption)
65          {
66              instance.Click(GetLocator(buttonCaption, buttonLocators));
67          }
68          public void PageReloadsInLessThanSeconds(String sec)
69          {
70              instance.WaitForPageToLoad(sec + "000");
71          }
72          public bool PageContainsText(String s)
73          {
74              return instance.IsTextPresent(s);
75          }
76          public bool PageURLIs(String s)
77          {
```

```
78          return s.Equals(instance.GetLocation());
79        }
80        public void UserSelectsFrom(String what, String where)
81        {
82            instance.Select(
83            GetLocator(where.Replace(" ", ""), selectLocators), what);
84        }
85      }
86  }
```

FitNesse Tests

HelloWorld

```
1    !define COMMAND_PATTERN {%m %p}
2    !define TEST_RUNNER {dotnet2\FitServer.exe}
3    !path D:\work\fitnesse\HelloWorld\bin\Release\HelloWorld.dll
4
5    !|HelloWorld.OurFirstTest|
6    |string1|string2|Concatenate?|
7    |Hello|World|Hello World|
```

InvoiceTable

```
1    !define COMMAND_PATTERN {%m %p}
2    !define TEST_RUNNER {dotnet2\FitServer.exe}
3    !path D:\work\fitnesse\extended\bin\Release\extended.dll
4
5
6    |import|
7    |extended|
8
9    !-
10   <table><tr><td colspan="3">Invoice</td></tr>
11   <tr><td>Item</td><td>Product code</td><td>Price</td></tr>
12   <tr><td>Pragmatic Programmer</td><td>B978-0201616224</td><td>34.03</
     td></tr>
13   <tr><td>Sony RDR-GX330</td><td>ERDR-GX330</td><td>94.80</td></tr>
14   <tr><td>Test Driven Development By Example</td><td>B978-0321146533</
     td><td>32.39</td></tr>
15   <tr><td>Net Total</td><td></td><td>161.22</td></tr>
16   <tr><td>Tax (10% on applicable items)</td><td></td><td>9.48</td></tr>
17   <tr><td>Total</td><td></td><td>170.70</td></tr>
18   </table>
19   -!
```

LoginTest

```
1   !|webfixture.WebTest|
2
3   !|Start Browser|*iehta|With Selenium Console On| localhost| At Port |
4444|And Scripts At|http://localhost:7711|
4
5   |User Opens URL|http://localhost:7711/login.aspx|
6   |User types|testuser|into|username|field|
7   |User types|testpassword|into|password|field|
8
9   |User clicks on|Log In|
10  |Page reloads in less than|3|seconds|
11  |Page contains text|You have logged in|
12
13  |Shutdown browser|
```

NicerPrizeCalculation

```
1   !define COMMAND_PATTERN {%m %p}
2   !define TEST_RUNNER {dotnet2\FitServer.exe}
3   !path D:\work\fitnesse\Tristan\bin\Release\Tristan.dll
4
5   !|Import|
6   |Tristan.Test|
7
8   The prize pool is divided among the winners using the following
 distribution for winning combinations (number of correct hits out of six
 chosen numbers). Example below is for $2M payout pool.
9
10  !|Prize Distribution for Payout Pool|2,000,000|
11  |Winning Combination|Pool Percentage?|Prize Pool?|
12  |6|68|1,360,000|
13  |5|10|200,000|
14  |4|10|200,000|
15  |3|12|240,000|
```

PlayerRegistrationFirstTry

```
1   !define COMMAND_PATTERN {%m %p}
2   !define TEST_RUNNER {dotnet2\FitServer.exe}
3   !path D:\work\fitnesse\Tristan\bin\Release\Tristan.dll
4
5   !|import|
6   |Tristan.Test|
7   |Tristan.Test.FirstTry|
```

```
8   !3 Upon registration, player details are stored correctly in the system,
    the player can log in, and the balance on his account is 0
9   !|Set Up Test Environment|
10
11  !|Player Registers|
12  |username|password|new player id?|
13  |johnsmith|test123|>>player|
14
15  !|Check Stored Details|
16  |player id|username?|balance?|
17  |<<player|johnsmith|0|
18
19  !|Check Log In|
20  |username|password|can log in?|
21  |johnsmith|test123|yes|
```

PlayerRegistrationSecondTry

```
1   !define COMMAND_PATTERN {%m %p}
2   !define TEST_RUNNER {dotnet2\FitServer.exe}
3   !path D:\work\fitnesse\Tristan\bin\Release\Tristan.dll
4
5   !|import|
6   |Tristan.Test|
7   |Tristan.Test.SecondTry|
8
9   !|Set Up Test Environment|
10  !3 Upon registration, player details are stored correctly in the system,
    the player can log in, and the balance on his account is 0
11  |Player Registers|
12  |username|password|name|address|city|postcode|country|new player id?|
13  |johnsmith|test123|John Smith|44 Ranelagh Way|London|NN1EE1|UK|>>player|
14
15  |Check Stored Details For |player|
16  |username?|name?|address?|city?|postcode?|country?|balance?|
17  |johnsmith|John Smith|44 Ranelagh Way|London|NN1EE1|UK|0|
18
19  |Check Log In|
20  |username|password|logged in as player id?|
21  |johnsmith|test123|<<player|
```

PlayerRegistrationThirdTry

```
1   !define COMMAND_PATTERN {%m %p}
2   !define TEST_RUNNER {dotnet2\FitServer.exe}
3   !path D:\work\fitnesse\Tristan\bin\Release\Tristan.dll
4
5   !|import|
```

```
6    |Tristan.Test|
7    |Tristan.Test.SecondTry|
8
9    |Set Up Test Environment|
10   !3 Player cannot register if the requested username already exists
11   |Player Registers|
12   |username|password|name|address|city|postcode|country|new player id?|
13   |johnsmith|test123|John Smith|44 Ranelagh Way|London|NN1EE1|UK|>>player|
14   |johnsmith|test334|Smith2|55 Ranelagh Way|London|NN2EE2|UK|
exception["Duplicate username"]|
15   !3 Player cannot log-in with an incorrect password
16   |Check Log In|
17   |username|password|logged in as player id?|
18   |johnsmith|test123|<<player|
19   |johnsmith|test334|exception["Invalid password"]|
```

PrizeCalculation

```
1    !define COMMAND_PATTERN {%m %p}
2    !define TEST_RUNNER {dotnet2\FitServer.exe}
3    !path D:\work\fitnesse\Tristan\bin\Release\Tristan.dll
4
5    !|Import|
6    |Tristan.Test|
7
8    !|Payout Table|
9    |Payout Pool|Winning Combination|Pool Percentage?|Prize Pool?|
10   |2,000,000|6|68|1,360,000|
11   |2,000,000|5|10|200,000|
12   |2,000,000|4|10|200,000|
13   |2,000,000|3|12|240,000|
```

PrizeCalculationFirstTry

```
1    !define COMMAND_PATTERN {%m %p}
2    !define TEST_RUNNER {dotnet2\FitServer.exe}
3    !path D:\work\fitnesse\Tristan\bin\Release\Tristan.dll
4    !|Tristan.Test.PayoutTable|
5    |payoutPool|winningCombination|PoolPercentage?|PrizePool?|
6    |2000000|6|68|1360000|
7    |2000000|5|10|200000|
8    |2000000|4|10|200000|
9    |2000000|3|12|240000|
```

PurchaseTicketFirstTry

```
1    !define COMMAND_PATTERN {%m %p}
```

```
2    !define TEST_RUNNER {dotnet2\FitServer.exe}
3    !path D:\work\fitnesse\Tristan\bin\Release\Tristan.dll
4
5    !|import|
6    |Tristan.Test.PurchaseTicket|
7
8    |Set Up Test Environment|
9    |Create Draw|
10   |01/01/2008|
11
12   |Player Registers|
13   |username|password|name|address|city|postcode|country|new player id?|
14   |john|test123|John Smith|44 Ranelagh Way|London|NN1EE1|UK|>>player|
15
16   !3 A player registers, transfers money into the account and purchases a
     ticket. The ticket should be registered for the correct draw in the system,
     and the account balance and pool size will be adjusted for the ticket value
17
18   |Purchase Ticket|
19   |Player|john|Deposits|100|dollars with card|4111111111111111|and expiry
     date|01/12|
20   |Player|john|has|100|dollars|
21   |Player|john|buys a ticket with numbers|1,3,4,5,8,10| for draw on |
     01/01/2008|
22   |Pool value for draw on |01/01/2008|is|10|dollars|
23   |Player|john|has|90|dollars|
24   |Ticket with numbers|1,3,4,5,8,10| for |10| dollars is registered for
     player|john| for draw on |01/01/2008|
```

PurchaseTicketNotEnoughMoney

```
1    !define COMMAND_PATTERN {%m %p}
2    !define TEST_RUNNER {dotnet2\FitServer.exe}
3    !path D:\work\fitnesse\Tristan\bin\Release\Tristan.dll
4
5    !|import|
6    |Tristan.Test.PurchaseTicket|
7
8    |Set Up Test Environment|
9    |Create Draw|
10   |01/01/2008|
11
12   |Player Registers|
13   |username|password|name|address|city|postcode|country|new player id?|
14   |john|test123|John Smith|44 Ranelagh Way|London|NN1EE1|UK|>>player|
15   !3 When there is not enough money in the account, the ticket purchase
     should be refused. The ticket should not be registered, account balance and
     pool value remain untouched.
```

```
16  |Purchase Ticket|
17  |Player|john|Deposits|50|dollars with card|4111111111111111|and expiry
date|01/12|
18  |reject|Player|john|buys|10| tickets with numbers|1,3,4,5,8,10| for draw
on |01/01/2008|
19  |Check|Pool value for draw on |01/01/2008|is|0|
20  |Check|Account balance for |john|50|
21  |Check|Tickets in draw on |01/01/2008|0|
22  |not|Ticket with numbers|1,3,4,5,8,10| for |100| dollars is registered
for player|john| for draw on |01/01/2008|
```

PurchaseTicketSecondTry

```
1   !define COMMAND_PATTERN {%m %p}
2   !define TEST_RUNNER {dotnet2\FitServer.exe}
3   !path D:\work\fitnesse\Tristan\bin\Release\Tristan.dll
4
5   !|import|
6   |Tristan.Test.PurchaseTicket|
7
8   |Set Up Test Environment|
9   |Create Draw|
10  |01/01/2008|
11
12  |Player Registers|
13  |username|password|name|address|city|postcode|country|new player id?|
14  |john|test123|John Smith|44 Ranelagh Way|London|NN1EE1|UK|>>player|
15  !3 A player registers, transfers money into the account and purchases a
ticket. The ticket should be registered for the correct draw in the system,
and the account balance and pool size will be adjusted for the ticket value
16  |Purchase Ticket|
17  |Player|john|Deposits|100|dollars with card|4111111111111111|and expiry
date|01/12|
18  |Player|john|has|100|dollars|
19  |Player|john|buys a ticket with numbers|1,3,4,5,8,10| for draw on |
01/01/2008|
20  |Check|Pool value for draw on |01/01/2008|is|10|
21  |Check|Account balance for |john|90|
22  |Ticket with numbers|1,3,4,5,8,10| for |10| dollars is registered for
player|john| for draw on |01/01/2008|
```

PurchaseTicketSuite.BasicCase

```
1   !3 A player registers, transfers money into the account and purchases a
ticket. The ticket should be registered for the correct draw in the system,
and the account balance and pool size will be adjusted for the ticket value
2   |Purchase Ticket|
```

```
3    |Player|john|Deposits|100|dollars with card|4111111111111111|and expiry
date|01/12|
4    |Player|john|has|100|dollars|
5    |Player|john|buys a ticket with numbers|1,3,4,5,8,10| for draw on |
01/01/2008|
6    |Check|Pool value for draw on |01/01/2008|is|10|
7    |Check|Account balance for |john|90|
8    |Ticket with numbers|1,3,4,5,8,10| for |10| dollars is registered for
player|john| for draw on |01/01/2008|
```

PurchaseTicketSuite.NotEnoughMoney

```
1    !3 When there is not enough money in the account, the ticket purchase
should be refused. The ticket should not be registered, account balance and
pool value remain untouched.
2    |Purchase Ticket|
3    |Player|john|Deposits|50|dollars with card|4111111111111111|and expiry
date|01/12|
4    |reject|Player|john|buys|10| tickets with numbers|1,3,4,5,8,10| for draw
on |01/01/2008|
5    |Check|Pool value for draw on |01/01/2008|is|0|
6    |Check|Account balance for |john|50|
7    |Check|Tickets in draw on |01/01/2008|0|
8    |not|Ticket with numbers|1,3,4,5,8,10| for |100| dollars is registered
for player|john| for draw on |01/01/2008|
```

PurchaseTicketSuite.SetUp

```
1    !|import|
2    |Tristan.Test.PurchaseTicket|
3
4    |Set Up Test Environment|
5    |Create Draw|
6    |01/01/2008|
7
8    |Player Registers|
9    |username|password|name|address|city|postcode|country|new player id?|
10   |john|test123|John Smith|44 Ranelagh Way|London|NN1EE1|UK|>>player|
```

PurchaseTicketSuite

```
1    !define COMMAND_PATTERN {%m %p}
2    !define TEST_RUNNER {dotnet2\FitServer.exe}
3    !path D:\work\fitnesse\Tristan\bin\Release\Tristan.dll
4
5    !contents -R
```

PurchaseTicketWithVariable

```
1    !define COMMAND_PATTERN {%m %p}
2    !define TEST_RUNNER {dotnet2\FitServer.exe}
3    !path D:\work\fitnesse\Tristan\bin\Release\Tristan.dll
4
5    !define username {john}
6
7    !|import|
8    |Tristan.Test.PurchaseTicket|
9
10   |Set Up Test Environment|
11   |Create Draw|
12   |01/01/2008|
13   |02/01/2008|
14
15   |Player Registers|
16   |username|password|name|address|city|postcode|country|new player id?|
17   |john|test123|John Smith|44 Ranelagh Way|London|NN1EE1|UK|>>player|
18   !3 A player registers, transfers money into the account and purchases a
     ticket. The ticket should be registered for the correct draw in the system,
     and the account balance and pool size will be adjusted for the ticket value
19   |Purchase Ticket|
20   |Player|${username}|Deposits|100|dollars with card|4111111111111111|and
     expiry date|01/12|
21   |Player|${username}|has|100|dollars|
22   |Player|${username}|buys a ticket with numbers|1,3,4,5,8,10| for |10|
     dollars for draw on |01/01/2008|
```

RegExHandler

```
1    !define COMMAND_PATTERN {%m %p}
2    !define TEST_RUNNER {dotnet2\FitServer.exe}
3    !path D:\work\fitnesse\extended\bin\Release\extended.dll
4
5
6    !|Cell Handler Loader|
7    |load|extended.RegExHandler|
8
9    !|StringFixture|
10   |field|field?|
11   |1938-111-222|/[0-9-]+/|
12   |1938-111-222|/[A-Z]+/|
```

SettlementTests.OneWinnerSixBallsFirstTry

```
1    !3 Arthur guessed all 6 balls correctly, so he takes the entire 6 out of
 6  prize
2
3    |Tickets in the Draw|
4    |player|numbers|value|
5    |Ford|2,11,22,33,39,18|50|
6    |Arthur|1,5,4,7,9,20|50|
7    |Trisha|10,21,30,6,16,26|50|
8    |Marvin|12,13,14,15,16,17|50|
9
10   |Draw results are|1,5,4,20,9,7|
11
12   |Accounts after the Draw|
13   |Player|Balance?|
14   |Arthur|118|
15   |Ford|50|
16   |Trisha|50|
17   |Marvin|50|
```

SettlementTests.SetUp

```
1    !|Tristan.Test.Settlement.SettlementTest|
2
3    |Accounts before the draw|
4    |player|balance|
5    |Arthur|100|
6    |Ford|100|
7    |Trisha|100|
8    |Marvin|100|
```

SettlementTests.TwoWinnersFourBalls

```
1    !3 Arthur and Trisha guess 4 balls correctly (1,5,4,20). Arthur bet 80
 dollars, Trisha bet 20, so the prize is split 4/1
2
3    |Tickets in the Draw|
4    |player|numbers|value|
5    |Ford|2,11,22,33,39,18|50|
6    |Arthur|1,5,4,7,9,20|80|
7    |Trisha|10,1,20,5,4,11|20|
8    |Marvin|12,13,14,15,16,17|50|
9
10   |Draw results are|1,5,4,20,38,37|
11
12   |Accounts after the Draw|
```

```
13   |Player|Balance?|
14   |Arthur|28|
15   |Ford|50|
16   |Trisha|82|
17   |Marvin|50|
```

SettlementTests

```
1    !define COMMAND_PATTERN {%m %p}
2    !define TEST_RUNNER {dotnet2\FitServer.exe}
3    !path D:\work\fitnesse\Tristan\bin\Release\Tristan.dll
4
5    !contents -R
```

TicketReviewTests.SetUp

```
1    !|Tristan.Test.ReviewTickets|
2
3    |Draw on |01/01/2008| is open|
4
5    |Player | john | opens account with | 100 | dollars|
```

TicketReviewTests.SeveralTicketsOneDraw

```
1    |Player|john|buys a ticket with numbers|1,3,4,5,8,10|for draw on|
01/01/2008|
2
3    |Player|john|buys a ticket with numbers|2,4,5,8,10,12|for draw on|
01/01/2008|
4
5    |Player|john|buys|5|tickets with numbers|3,6,9,12,15,18|for draw on|
01/01/2008|
6
7    |Player|john|lists open tickets|
8    |draw|numbers|value|
9    |01/01/2008|1,3,4,5,8,10|10|
10   |01/01/2008|2,4,5,8,10,12|10|
11   |01/01/2008|3,6,9,12,15,18|50|
```

TicketReviewTests.SeveralTicketsTwoDraws

```
1    |Draw on|02/01/2008|is open|
2
3    |Draw on|03/01/2008|is open|
4
```

```
5    |Player|john|buys a ticket with numbers|1,3,4,5,8,10|for draw on|
02/01/2008|
6
7    |Player|john|buys a ticket with numbers|1,3,4,5,8,10|for draw on|
01/01/2008|
8
9    |Player|john|buys|5|tickets with numbers|3,6,9,12,15,18|for draw on|
01/01/2008|
10
11   |Player|john|lists tickets for draw on|01/01/2008|
12   |value|numbers|
13   |10|1,3,4,5,8,10|
14   |50|3,6,9,12,15,18|
15
16   |Player|john|lists tickets for draw on|02/01/2008|
17   |value|numbers|
18   |10|1,3,4,5,8,10|
19
20   |Player|john|lists tickets for draw on|03/01/2008|
21   |value|numbers|
```

TicketReviewTests.TwoAccountsOneDraw

```
1    |Player|tom|opens account with|50|dollars|
2
3    |Player|john|buys a ticket with numbers|1,3,4,5,8,10|for draw on|
01/01/2008|
4
5    |Player|tom|buys a ticket with numbers|2,4,5,8,10,12|for draw on|
01/01/2008|
6
7    |Player|john|lists tickets for draw on|01/01/2008|
8    |value|numbers|
9    |10|1,3,4,5,8,10|
10
11   |Player|tom|lists tickets for draw on|01/01/2008|
12   |value|numbers|
13   |10|2,4,5,8,10,12|
```

TicketReviewTests.WinningsRecordedCorrectly

```
1    |Draw on|02/01/2008|is open|
2
3    |Player|john|buys a ticket with numbers|1,3,4,5,8,10|for draw on|
01/01/2008|
4
5    |Player|john|buys a ticket with numbers|1,3,4,5,8,10|for draw on|
02/01/2008|
```

```
6
7    |Player|john|buys|5|tickets with numbers|3,6,9,12,15,18|for draw on|
01/01/2008|
8
9    |Numbers|1,3,4,5,31,32|are drawn on|01/01/2008|
10
11   |Player|john|lists tickets for draw on|01/01/2008|
12   |value|numbers|is open|winnings|
13   |10|1,3,4,5,8,10|false|3|
14   |50|3,6,9,12,15,18|false|0|
15
16   |Player|john|lists open tickets|
17   |draw|value|numbers|
18   |02/01/2008|10|1,3,4,5,8,10|
```

TicketReviewTests

```
1    !define COMMAND_PATTERN {%m %p}
2    !define TEST_RUNNER {dotnet2\FitServer.exe}
3    !path D:\work\fitnesse\Tristan\bin\Release\Tristan.dll
4
5    !contents -R
```

TicketReviewTestsWithRowFixture

```
1    !define COMMAND_PATTERN {%m %p}
2    !define TEST_RUNNER {dotnet2\FitServer.exe}
3    !path D:\work\fitnesse\Tristan\bin\Release\Tristan.dll
4
5    !|Tristan.Test.ReviewTicketsWithRowFixture|
6
7    |Draw on |01/01/2008| is open|
8
9    |Player | john | opens account with | 100 | dollars|
10
11   |Player|john| buys a ticket with numbers |1,3,4,5,8,10 | for draw on |
01/01/2008|
12
13   |Player|john| buys a ticket with numbers |2,4,5,8,10,12 | for draw on |
01/01/2008|
14
15   |Player|john| buys |  5 | tickets with numbers |3,6,9,12,15,18 | for
draw on |01/01/2008|
16
17   |Player|john| lists open tickets |
18   |draw|numbers|value?|
19   |01/01/2008|1,3,4,5,8,10|10|
```

```
20   |01/01/2008|2,4,5,8,10,12|11|
21   |01/01/2008|3,6,9,12,15,18|50|
```

Build scripts

scripts/runfitnesse.build

```
1    <project default="test">
2    <property name="fitnesse.dir" value="c:\services\fitnesse" />
3    <property name="fitnesse.server" value="localhost" />
4    <property name="fitnesse.port" value="8888" />
5    <target name="test">
6     <exec program="${fitnesse.dir}\dotnet2\TestRunner.exe"
7      commandline="${fitnesse.server} ${fitnesse.port} ${fitnesse.test}"
8      workingdir="${fitnesse.dir}"/>
9    </target>
10   <target name="test">
11     <echo message="running tests ${fitnesse.test}" />
12     <delete file="${output.file}" />
13     <delete file="${format.file}" />
14     <exec program="${fitnesse.dir}\dotnet2\TestRunner.exe"
15      commandline="-results ${output.file} ${fitnesse.server}
      ${fitnesse.port} ${fitnesse.test}"
16      workingdir="${fitnesse.dir}"
17      failonerror="true"/>
18     <echo message="tests ${fitnesse.test} complete" />
19   </target>
20   <target name="format">
21     <echo message="formatting ${fitnesse.test} results" />
22     <delete file="${format.file}" />
23     <exec program="java.exe"
24      workingdir="${fitnesse.dir}"
25      commandline="-cp ${fitnesse.dir}\fitnesse.jar
      fitnesse.runner.FormattingOption ${output.file} xml ${format.file}
      ${fitnesse.server} ${fitnesse.port} ${fitnesse.test}" failonerror="false"/>
26     <echo message="formatting ${fitnesse.test} results into ${format.file}
      complete" />
27   </target>
28   </project>
```

scripts/ccnet.config

```
1    <cruisecontrol>
2    <project name="Continuous-Test">
3     <workingDirectory>w:\ccnetbuild\source\test</workingDirectory>
4     <artifactDirectory>w:\ccnetbuild\artifact-cont\test</artifactDirectory>
```

```
5    <tasks>
6    <exec>
7     <executable>net.exe</executable>
8     <buildArgs>stop ccnetfitnesse</buildArgs>
9    </exec>
10   <exec>
11    <executable>net.exe</executable>
12    <buildArgs>start ccnetfitnesse</buildArgs>
13   </exec>
14   <nant>
15      <buildFile>w:\ccnetbuild\source\build\runfitnesse.build</buildFile>

16      <buildTimeoutSeconds>300000</buildTimeoutSeconds>
17      <buildArgs>-D:output.file=c:\temp\fitnesse-tx.log -D:format.file=c:
\temp\fitnesse-tx.xml -D:fitnesse.test=TicketReviewTests</buildArgs>
18      <targetList><target>test</target></targetList>
19   </nant>
20   </tasks>
21   <publishers>
22   <nant>
23      <buildFile>w:\ccnetbuild\source\build\runfitnesse.build</buildFile>

24      <buildTimeoutSeconds>300000</buildTimeoutSeconds>
25      <buildArgs>-D:output.file=c:\temp\fitnesse-tx.log -D:format.file=c:
\temp\fitnesse-tx.xml -D:fitnesse.test=TicketReviewTests</buildArgs>
26      <targetList><target>format</target></targetList>
27   </nant>
28    <merge>
29            <files>
30                <file>c:\temp\fitnesse-tx.xml</file>
31            </files>
32        </merge>
33    <xmllogger />
34   </publishers>
35  </project>
36 </cruisecontrol>
```

Web code

code/testsite/loginform.html

```
1   <html>
2   <body>
3    <form method="post" action="login.aspx">
4    <table>
5    <tr><td>Username:</td><td><input type="text" name="username" /></td></
tr>
```

```
6      <tr><td>Password:</td><td><input type="password" name="password" /></
td></tr>
7      <tr><td><input type="submit" name="login" value="Log In"/></td><td></
td></tr>
8      </table>
9      </form>
10   </body>
11   </html>
```

code/testsite/login.aspx

```
1    <%@PAGE Language="C#"%>
2    <%
3    //just a dummy page to act as an endpoint for selenium tests
4    //will authorise testuser with testpassword, and decline everyone else
5    if (!String.IsNullOrEmpty(Request["username"])){
6      if ("testuser".Equals(Request["username"]) &&
7        "testpassword".Equals(Request["password"])){
8        Response.Write ("You have logged in");
9      }
10     else {
11       Response.Write ("Error: username or password incorrect");
12     }
13   }
14   else{
15     Response.Redirect("loginform.html");
16   }
17   %>
```

Index

Symbols

${}$ 76
<< 49
>> 49

A

AbstractCellHandler class 158
acceptance test
  compared to unit test 32
  introduced 31
  who should write them? 31
Accessor class 155
ActionFixture class 67
ajax, testing with Selenium 131
Args array 43
arguments 43
array
  automatic conversion 63, 86
  automatic wrapping with DoFixture 96
  strings or ints 98
ArrayFixture class 96
  compared with RowFixture 101
  converting result to test 146
automated acceptance testing 31
automated build tool 107
  scheduling tests 119

B

Bathyscaphe Trieste 34
blank
  cell 56, 144
  keyword 56
BoolFixture class 52
BoundFixture class 154
bound variable 140
bug, exterminating 35

build script, source code 214
business analyst
  involvement in testing 8, 29, 31, 37, 42, 46
  writing tests without learning wiki syntax 144
business domain object 52, 90, 145
business form, use as test 147
business object 145, 167
  collection 96
  FIT hooks 16
business rule
  and acceptance test 79
  and test suite 72
  testing directly 78
  testing through the UI 121

C

C# classes, source code 175
CamelCase
  automatic conversion into links 20
  valid page names 22
cell handler
  custom 158
  DoFixture and ActionFixture 68
  EndsWithHandler 157, 157
  implementation 154
  IntegralRangeHandler 157
  loading on demand 157
  non-standard 157
  RegExHandler 159
  StartsWithHandler 157
  SubstringHandler 157
  using with FitLibrary 155
  with DoFixture 155
CellHandlerLoader class 157
CellOperation class 154
cell operation handler (see cell handler)
central server 107

217

Printed in the United Kingdom
by Lightning Source UK Ltd.
131034UK00001B/289/P